Ocracoke Wild

A Naturalist's Year on an Outer Banks Island

With Illustrations and Photographs by the Author

2006
Parkway Publishers, Inc.
Boone, North Carolina

First printing May, 1995
Second Printing 2006

Library of Congress Cataloging-in-Publication Data

Garber, Pat.
Ocracoke wild : a naturalist's year on an Outer Banks island / Pat
Garber; with illustrations and photographs by the author.
p. cm.
Originally published: Asheboro, NC: Down Home Press, 1995. [With a
new foreword and reviews}.
ISBN 1-933251-3 1-X
I. Natural history--North Carolina--Ocracoke Island. 2. Ocracoke Island
(N.C.)--Description and travel. 3. Garber, Pat. I. Title.
QHI05.N8G38 2006
508.756'184--dc22 2006045353

Cover Painting by Pat Garber
Book design concept by Katrina Breitenbach
Cover Design by Gina Cavallaro

The material in this book originally appeared, in different form,
in the *Island Breeze* of Hatteras-Ocracoke.

Parkway Publishers, Inc.
PO Box 3678
Boone, NC 28607
http://www.parkwaypublishers.com

For Duchess, my Doberman companion and friend, who was with me through all my years at Ocracoke, and is buried now under a windswept dune overlooking the sea.

Acknowledgements

Thanks to Irene Nolan and Tony MacGowan of the *Island Breeze*, without whom this collection would not exist; to the rangers of the National Park Service, who made possible many of the experiences described in this collection; to my many good friends at Ocracoke, some of whom are mentioned in these stories and all of whom have given me invaluable support; and most of all, to my parents, who taught me to love all of nature and to follow my dreams, wherever they lead me.

Contents

Summer

Fall

Foreword

It has been eleven years since *Ocracoke Wild* was published, and even longer since the essays were first written for my "Sea to Sound" column in the *Island Breeze*. Many things have changed since then; in the world, on the island, in my own life. Some of these changes are documented in my second book, *Ocracoke Odyssey*, published in 1999, but incredible events have reshaped the world even since then. The tragedy of 9/11, wars in Afghanistan and Iraq, tsunamis and deadly hurricanes have rocked the world. Closer home are the race to develop Ocracoke Island, the loss of my parents and other loved ones, and the natural transitions that accompany eleven years of aging.

Re-reading the essays in *Ocracoke Wild*, I realize that most of these episodes could have taken place yesterday. The rhythms of nature are timeless. Sea turtles still return to the same beaches to lay their eggs; brown pelicans still soar in formations above the sea; fiddler crabs still burrow along the edge of the salt marsh, just as they did when I wrote about them, just as they did a thousand years ago. Perhaps it is this sense of continuity, of congruity in a changing, incongruous world that makes preserving these wonders of nature so important. It is my hope that reading this collection of essays will create in its readers a feeling of connection with the natural world and a commitment to protect and cherish its treasures.

Ocracoke Wild Reviews

"As we follow Garber through the pages of "Ocracoke Wild," we almost smell the sea, the sun-lured fragrance of myrtle bushes, feel the sand underfoot, the tickle of sea oats and the sting of the surf upon our legs. This is a book for all beach-lovers, and it will make beach lovers of those of us who have not yet succumbed." -- *Mae Woods Bell, the Rocky Mount Telegram*

"(It) reads more like letters to a friend than a scientific treatise and is sure to delight lovers of nature and Ocracoke." -- *Richmond Magazine*

"[Pat Garber,] the environmental anthropologist ruminates as she holds a dragonfly during a kayak trip, recalls a childhood pet blue crab, endures a night rain to spot toads, and marvels at bioluminescent protozoans glowing on her boat's anchor line." -- *Southern Living*

"Garber needles us out of our numbness to nature. This happens again and again, as she describes wild ponies, piping plovers, and snowy egrets." -- *Bill Ruehlmann, Norfolk Virginian Pilot*

"Throughout the book, [Pat Garber's] message to the reader is that we share in the responsibility to protect the wildlife, marshes, beaches, and quality of the natural island system. These are the real treasures." -- *Coastwatch*

Introduction

Ocracoke Island is a narrow strip of sand, marsh, and woods lying off the coast of North Carolina. It is part of the Outer Banks, a series of barrier islands that protect the mainland from the worst of the ocean's storms. Like the other islands, Ocracoke is at the mercy of the wind and the sea, and in response, it is constantly changing shape and moving. It is seventeen miles long and seldom more than a mile wide, a silver ribbon marking the horizon between the restless ocean and the endless sky.

On the high ground at the southwest end of the island lies the village of Ocracoke. Originally the home of Croatan Indians arid later of English pilots who guided ships through the inlet in the 1600s, it has a history of pirates, seafarers, and fishermen, Approximately 700 people live there today coexisting with the herons and the bluefish, the tree frogs and the mosquitoes, the wind and the sea.

I knew that I wanted to live at Ocracoke within the first hour that I set foot there. I was on my way to Virginia, hitchhiking north from a summer spent crewing on sailboats in the Bahamas. I immediately fell in love with the long, undeveloped seashore, the elusive marshes, and the picturesque fishing village strung around Silver Lake Harbor.

Within the second hour, I had found myself a job cleaning motel rooms and a campsite for my tent. I was not discouraged by the hordes of mosquitoes that descended on my tent each night, nor by the hurricane that closed down the island within the first month that I was there.

Before long, I had rented a little cottage in the marshes at the end of a long, sandy lane. I bought an old Pontiac Sunbird, which soon proved to be a mistake. I knocked the muffler off the first time I tried to drive it on the beach, and put a hole in the radiator in the sandy ruts of the road leading to my house. When I found out that the engine was shot as well, I semi-retired it and got myself a used beach bike.

This turned out to be a much better deal. Mary Jane, as I named it, carried me all over the island, down sandy lanes and through flooded streets, both day and night. With it and my 12-foot sailboat, the Kittiwake, I could explore the whole island.

I brought down my Siamese cat from Virginia, and we were soon joined by Duchess, a six-month-old, red-and-tan Doberman pinscher, who loved to splash in the surf and chase ghost crabs. Together, we settled in for a cold, windy winter in the salt marsh.

I was suffering the aftermath of a painful divorce, and the lonely primitive life we led was what I needed. With only a small kerosene stove for heat, we all hunkered down under piles of blankets as the cold northeast winds swept around us. I washed clothes using a hand-operated wringer washing machine.

A newly found fisherman friend gave me a 30-foot-long gill net, and another loaned me a crab pot. I set them out in Pamlico Sound, not far from where I lived, and I used my sailboat to fish them. I always had fresh fish on my table, though not always your traditional restaurant fare. Not wanting to waste anything I caught, I tried a lot of creative, sometimes dubious, methods to prepare sand sharks, skates, and whatever else blundered into my net. I also collected clams, oysters, and mussels, all of which were within wading distance of my house.

In the spring, I planted a garden, but a high spring tide destroyed everything except the tomatoes, which were planted on higher ground. In honor of Euell Gibbons, I tried all sorts of ways to prepare seaweed, but was not overly impressed. Later on, when the summer shrimp boats started pulling into South Point Fish

House, I got a job heading shrimp, and brought home the broken pieces to sauté in butter.

I walked the ocean beaches with my dog Duchess; I sailed the creeks and shallows of the sound in my little sailboat; I spent hours sitting in the swing on my porch, strumming my guitar. I painted, I wrote, and I healed. In the fall, a year after I had first come to Ocracoke, I accepted a long-coveted teaching position with the Havasupai Indian Tribe in the Grand Canyon of Arizona. Sadly bidding Ocracoke goodbye, Duchess and I set out on our new adventure, but we promised to return.

We did, five years later, in the spring of 1991. While in Arizona I had completed a graduate degree in environmental anthropology, and I was anxious to incorporate it into my life. I pursued an idea I had discussed earlier with Tony Sylvester, the owner of the surf shop, Ride the Wind.

Using his open kayaks, I began conducting environmental kayak  tours through the salt marshes. I completed my training to become a state and federally licensed wildlife rehabilitator and began working with the injured and orphaned birds of the island. I became a VIP--Volunteer in the Park--with the National Park Service, participating in the programs they conducted with nesting sea turtles, migratory shorebirds, and the formerly wild Ocracoke ponies. I took every opportunity I could find to be out in the marshes or on the sea, learning more about Ocracoke and its wild inhabitants.

That winter, I began writing a nature column, "From Sea to Sound," for the Hatteras-Ocracoke publication, the Island Breeze. The experiences I had known living with the wild things of Ocracoke became the basis for my stories. Some were joyful, others heartbreakingly sad. All of them had something to teach me.

Duchess died of cancer in the fall of '93, leaving an empty spot in my house and in my heart. My two cats and a variety of transient hospitalized birds were still with me, though. By this time, I was spending part of my time on a 28-foot Cape Dory sailboat, the Aurora, with a good friend. I continued to write while sailing the Chesapeake Bay and the sounds and rivers of North Carolina. After winning several state and national awards for my column, and at the urging of a number of people, I decided to put the stories together and publish them as a book. I hope that they give you even a small sense of all that the wild things of Ocracoke have given me.

Winter

Pamlico Sound:
The Mother of Life

At Ocracoke's western boundary, one can gaze along the island's winding shoreline and across wide, still waters to the mainland. Creeks rich with ribbed mussels and oysters divide the marshlands into a jigsaw puzzle as they wind into the shallow waters of the tidal flats, where hermit crabs, disguised in the shells of whelks and moonshells, scurry about. Here, at low tide, one can gather hard-shelled clams using just feet and toes to find them.

A little farther out, a bed of eel grass makes a dark shadow in the water. It is home to bay scallops, blue crabs, and many species of fish fry. In the distance, snowy egrets and a great blue heron quietly stalk their dinner, proof that the shallows extend deceptively far out into the dark waters. Diamondback terrapins, skates, and flounder glide silently along the silted bottom there.

The depth of the water eventually increases, reaching 15 feet and providing thoroughfares for fishing boats and ferries, and habitat for all kinds of sharks, shrimp, bony fish, and loons. The waters seem to fade into the horizon, eventually reaching the mainland shore.

This is the Pamlico Sound, one of the largest bodies of water on the East Coast. Rich with a wide variety of animal and plant life, it has provided a bountiful living for people along its shores for thousands of years. It is the mother of life for Ocracoke and other North Carolina barrier islands.

I was skimming across the Pamlico's surface, enjoying the varied beauty of the sound, sitting at the stern of my newly acquired 13-foot Lazer sailboat. I had christened her the *Kittiwake II*, in fond memory of the first sailboat I had owned. It was a chill February day, but I was bundled in a wool hat, a heavy sweatshirt, and rain gear. The wind was blowing out of the southeast at a gentle 10 to 15 knots—perfect since I was still not quite used to handling the boat. I soared across the water with the wind behind me.

As I glided along, I thought about another impressive body of water—the Chesapeake Bay of Virginia and Maryland. I had spent the summer sailing the bay waters on a 28-foot sloop, enjoying the lazy rivers that pour their hearts into her wide shallow belly; the picturesque towns, full of colorful sailboats and dignified old deadrisers; and the lovely little islands that quietly grow and erode away in her shallow waters. As a native Virginian, I had felt like a prodigal daughter returning home.

But everywhere I went on that laconic voyage, my joy was tempered with sadness. I constantly saw reminders that the mighty Chesapeake was but a shadow of her former self. Museums reveled in stories of her earlier days, when she was the oyster capital of the world and skipjacks plied her waters, but mourned the fact that those days were long gone. Watermen worried about their livelihoods as oyster, crab, and fish catches plummeted each year. "Save the Bay" signs adorned car bumpers and, in shop windows, books and magazines lamented the sorry state of the bay today. My sailing companion and I were disappointed to find that we were unable to live off her bounty as we had planned.

On the positive side, an incredibly widespread, well-funded, and dedicated movement is in progress to restore the Chesapeake. The movement includes people in agriculture, industry, development, government, and most importantly, average citizens—all the Virginians and Marylanders who love the bay. I wish them success with all my heart.

As I adjusted my sail, keeping the wind behind me, I thought about the dark waters through which I was now gliding. Things haven't gotten quite that bad in North Carolina yet. Pamlico Sound is still a relatively healthy estuary, but unless protective measures are taken, it will not continue to be.

Among all the different perspectives on the Chesapeake, there is a consensus that had the "Save the Bay" movement started earlier, the job would have been a lot easier. It makes sense for North Carolina to take a lesson from her sister states and begin cleaning up her estuary waters now.

The elements that have contributed to destroying the health of the Chesapeake Bay are widespread, starting hundreds of miles inland, even in other states. These include pesticides and fertilizers used on farms in rural Pennsylvania, industrial gases released from smokestacks in Baltimore, sewage systems in the suburbs of Washington, D.C., and chemical waste from paper mills in West Point, Virginia.

Similar factors are affecting Pamlico Sound. In order to protect the fisheries at Ocracoke, it is necessary to address problems hundreds of miles inland as well as at the shoreline. Most of the pollution threatening the sound is carried by rivers from farms, cities, and factories on the mainland.

It was originally believed that most pollution came from factories and sewage systems that released contaminants directly into the estuaries. These pollutants, known as point sources, are now regulated by the Clean Water Act and the Clean Air Act, however, and their impact has been reduced. It is the contaminants that are widespread and difficult to pinpoint, known as non-point sources, that are the biggest problem today.

Fertilizers and pesticides from agricultural areas wash into ditches and creeks, eventually reaching rivers and finally Pamlico Sound. Nitrates contained in the fertilizers cause algal blooms that use up the oxygen supply in the water, killing native grasses and the life that depends on them. Herbicides and insecticides poison the fish and contaminate the shellfish, working their way up the food chain to all species.

Residents of cities, suburbs, and small towns located near waterways have an impact on the sound as well. When trees are cut to build homes, shopping centers, and roads, an important provider of erosion and pollution control is removed. Each time a wooded lot is cleared for development, an open path is provided for silt and contaminants to enter the nearest stream or river. When roads are cut and paved, this path becomes a channel leading ultimately to the coast.

Heavy metals, which are extremely toxic in even the smallest quantities, are released into the environment when roads and tunnels are dug through rock beds. When they reach rivers and sounds, they cause fish kills and other environmental damage, often without being detected.

Even ordinary household activities add to the pollution, particularly when you live near a watershed. Changing automobile oil in the driveway, fertilizing the lawn, rinsing out a can of paint or paint thinner in the yard, spraying a nest of ants—all of these actions have the potential of adding to the pollution in Pamlico Sound.

Residents along the sound bear particular responsibility. Because we live so close to the water, everything we do has an impact on it. Septic systems, particularly for older homes and motels, sometimes discharge into creeks that lead into the sound. Old car and boat engines leach oil or antifreeze into the ground and eventually into the water. Boaters with heads, or bathrooms, on board sometimes avoid the high cost of pump-out stations by discharging the effluent into the water.

Trash tossed onto the roads, pulled out of trash containers by dogs, or carelessly left in yards is washed into the sound during storms and high tides. Boaters sometimes throw oil cans, plastic bags, and other things over the sides. This trash ends up littering the beaches, or worse, being eaten by sea turtles or whales, which die as a result.

Many of our food fish and shellfish are declining, not only as a result of pollution and development, but also because of overfishing. In the past, destructive fishing methods and lack of regulation have harmed not only the fisheries but also the industries dependent on them. Solutions are being sought by fishermen, scientists, and government regulators, but there are no clear-cut answers. Fin fish, sharks, crabs, oysters and other shellfish are all species at risk in North Carolina's estuary waters.

As a result of all these causes, Ocracoke's Silver Lake and Oyster Creek are no longer safe for shellfish collection. Oysters and clams, which filter and accumulate toxins, are the miners' canaries of the sea. They warn us of encroaching danger. When the waters of the sound are no longer safe for them, we know that they are also unsafe for us.

I was scheduled to give a guitar lesson in two hours, so it was time for me to head back to shore. Pushing hard on the tiller, I came about and started back. It would be a slower trek this time, since I had to tack back and forth against the wind. As I skimmed along over the ebony surface, I said a silent prayer for the well-being of this great body of water.

I knew that protecting Pamlico Sound and the rest of North Carolina's coastal waters ultimately would depend on me, along with all the other people who love and rely on their beauty and their bounty. I hoped that we would be up to the job.

❧

The Message of the Sea Horse

Walking on the beach one day, I found a treasure. It was the morning after a winter storm—a "nor'easter"—and the sand was still wet from the swells that had washed over it at high tide, littering it with debris: broken shells, pieces of driftwood, clumps of seaweed, and an occasional piece of Styrofoam or broken glass.

My mind was drifting elsewhere as I strode along, not really paying attention to where I was walking. But suddenly it was there, directly before my eye's path, and in that great stretch of ocean litter, it seemed like a jewel waiting just for me.

Tiny and fragile, a perfect sea horse lay dried into an almost circular coil. It wasn't more than an inch across, light as a feather and exquisitely formed.

Where did it come from? How did it die? How did its fragile perfection survive the stormy seas, the voracious predators, the incredible journey it must have undergone to wash up on this beach today?

Sea horses, known by the scientific name *Hippocampus*, are one of the most unusual kinds of fish. Their scales are forged into ridged, armor-like plates. They swim upright, using their dorsal and pectoral fins; but they are not strong swimmers. They spend their summers clinging with their tails to the blades of eel or turtle grass that grow in sheltered bays from New Hampshire to Florida. Where they go in the winter is a mystery.

Sea horses mate when they are about two years old. Males and females find each other by means of clicking sounds they make by snapping their necks. The female deposits her eggs in a pouch on the abdomen of the male. The eggs hatch in about 25 days, and the tiny infant sea horses swim into the ocean, sometimes returning to their father's pouch for protection until they are older.

As they cling to the blades of seaweed, the sea horses inflate the sides of their heads and suck in small organisms that float by. Young ones consume plankton, while adults eat small crustaceans, fish eggs, and other minute creatures. They in turn are eaten by a number of kinds of fish. People do not normally eat sea horses, but the Chinese grind them up to use as medicine.

While most sea horses live among the grasses of sheltered waters, some attach themselves to pieces of floating sargassum weed. They join the great mass of floating plants and animals that drift through the Gulf Stream,

traveling sometimes as far away as Europe or the Sargasso Sea.

These are the facts about sea horses. But as I stood on the ocean shore hold- ing my tiny trea- sure, I wondered what sea horses were really like. I tried to imagine living my life among the strands of eelgrass, watching the world through an undulating, blue-green window of sea water and trying to hide in the shadowy recesses when the silhouette of a hungry fish draws near. Conceiving and delivering 100 or more offspring at a time; then watching them swim away, perhaps to be devoured by predators, or swallowed up and lost in the vast expanses of endless water. Swaying gently through life, rocked by the hypnotic motion of the moon-driven waves; or tossed violently about as a storm thunders through the whitecaps above—always subject to the whims of the mighty seas.

Was my sea horse content with his destiny, never questioning or wondering why? Or did he wonder what lay beyond the liquid world surrounding him? Did he dream of faraway lands? Long to feel the warmth of the sun, to see the shimmering light of distant stars?

Perhaps he was an adventurer, abandoning the safety of sheltered bays to grasp a strand of drifting seaweed and cast his lot with the waves. Maybe he was a messenger sent by King Neptune, and had traveled hundreds of miles and encountered untold adventures before destiny dealt him a last fatal blow and delivered him to my hand.

Turning homeward, I cradled the sea horse reverently in my palm, trying to understand the message he had brought me.

Bewhiskered Clown:
The Harbor Seal

It was dusk as we bounced across the beach in Mickey and George Roberson's four-wheel drive, the end of a cold, bleak, and rainy January afternoon. A nor'easter had arrived the day before, and the gale-force winds and 12-foot seas had not completely subsided. The air, heavy with the makings of a soon-to-come downpour, was chilling, and the wind whistled around us.

But our thoughts were not on the weather as we approached South Point, that amorphous spit of shifting sand where the Atlantic Ocean meets Pamlico Sound. We were staring at a dark blob floating in the water, a sight that was unfamiliar to all of us. As we drew nearer, the blob gradually became a shape; then it materialized into a living creature—a harbor seal.

A comical looking creature with a spotted, three-foot-long body, it bounced in the ripples of the shallow sound waters, with its bewhiskered, old-man's face protruding above the surface. Its eyes were closed, and we soon realized that it was asleep.

On a beach in Massachusetts or California, this might not have been an unusual sight, but this was Ocracoke. None of us had ever seen a seal along this coastline, and a few years ago, it would have been unheard of. Recently, however, there had been an increasing number of sightings of harbor seals along the Outer Banks. Scientists speculate that they are being pushed southward by food shortages and possibly by cold water in their traditional territories. Most of the seals that have washed up on beaches here have been young. Some have been sick or dead, the victims of net and boat injuries and illnesses likely related to pollution. As their numbers increase, however, it appears that harbor seals are becoming a permanent fixture in North Carolina's marine landscape.

Harbor seals are one of the species of marine mammals classified as "true seals," which lack external ears. Hind flippers which point backwards make them extremely agile in the water but slow and awkward on land. They live in both the Atlantic and Pacific Oceans, inhabiting coastal shallows and harbor mouths, as their name implies. Principally fish eaters, these seals also feed on mollusks and crustaceans. They in turn become food for sharks and, in northern waters, killer whales and polar bears.

The harbor seals that have been showing up on North Carolina's beaches probably breed and raise their young on rocky beaches north of New Hampshire. The pups are born in late spring on the Atlantic coastline between the high tides. They are precocious and soon join their mothers on swimming expeditions, but continue to nurse for about three weeks. The parents, usually monogamous, mate again about three weeks later.

Seals, along with other marine mammals, have been ruthlessly hunted in the past for furs, oil, and sometimes meat. Today, they are protected by the Marine Mammal Protection Act of 1972, but large numbers still die as "incidental catch" in fishing nets, particularly on the northwest coast. Always an important part of the Eskimo economy, they are still taken in limited numbers by these and other indigenous people in Alaska.

Many people know harbor seals best as the residents of zoos and aquariums, where they become quite tame and perform simple "tricks" for their trainers. They are intelligent animals and seem to enjoy the company of humans. Whether it is right to keep them in captivity for economic gain, however, is an ethical question being addressed by animal rights advocates. I prefer to see them in the ocean or on beaches where they can roam wild and free.

The arrival of harbor seals in North Carolina reminds us that the natural world is not static. It continues to change, just as it has for millions of years. As some animals disappear from their traditional ranges, others appear. Is human development, over-fishing, or pollution driving these seals south to our beaches, or is this immigration part of a natural ecological process? Indeed, in the long-term view, is there a difference?

Whatever the case, I welcome the arrival of these elegant, funny-looking clowns to Ocracoke.

The Plankton:
A World in a Drop of Water

I had just returned from a kayak trip through the tidal flats. As I waded through the molasses-like mud of the creek, ready to haul my kayak up on the bank, an acquaintance from the village walked up.

"Did you see much life out there?" she asked.

I shook my head. "Maybe it's too early. The diamondback terrapins are probably still asleep, and there weren't many birds. Didn't even see many fish. Not much out there today."

Even as I spoke, a subconscious voice reprimanded me.

Is that true?

Maybe I didn't *see* much out there, but did that mean it wasn't there?

The sound—even the creek where I was now standing—actually was swarming with life. I reached down and scooped up a handful of water. Thousands of minute plants and animals were there, all engaged in the business of staying alive and providing life for other creatures.

Not only was there life out there, but also the foundation of all other life—the plankton—was there, invisible to my limited eyesight but utterly necessary to my existence.

Plankton is the drifting mass of microscopic organisms, both free-swimming and suspended, that live in the earth's great bodies of water. The term comes from the Greek word for wanderer, for planktonic life forms, both plant and animal, move with the currents and the winds. Plankton is composed of two forms: *Holoplankton*, which spend their entire lives in the plankton, and *Meroplankton*, which live there only in their larval stages.

Planktonic organisms are more prolific in shallow coastal waters than in the ocean depths, and most are located near the surface. Although the organisms cannot be seen individually by the naked eye, waters rich in plankton can be distinguished by their green color, a combination of blue light waves reflected by the water and yellow light waves from the plankton. Beautiful though they may be, great expanses of azure water are generally liquid deserts, devoid of life. Green water, on the other hand, suggests a jungle of underwater life.

One-celled protozoa, which are the most numerous organisms in the plankton, are believed to have been the first life form on earth. They have been drifting in the seas for 570 million years, unchanged since the Cambrian times. They are part of the Holoplankton, spending their whole lives in this state. They move by three methods: some produce motion by beating long extensions called flagella; others move by the synchronous beat of numerous cilia; and some by extruding protoplasmic appendages into which the rest of the body flows.

Microscopic plants, known as Phytoplankton, could be considered the foundation of all life. It is claimed that they account for 75 to 85 percent of the organic rnatter and 80 percent of the oxygen produced on earth. They are the basis of the ocean's food chain, making up what is known as the primary trophic, or feeding, level. They include one celled diatoms, dinoflagellates, and other minute algae. They are found in the upper layers of the sea, where they can absorb sunlight for photosynthesis, through which they create most of the energy that is eventually dispensed throughout the seas.

Diatoms, a yellow-green algae, are formed of two halves which fit together, giving them their name, which means "cut in two" in Greek. They are probably the most numerous and important food source in the plankton. According to Robert Hendrickson's *Ocean Almanac*, it takes 10,000 pounds of diatoms, working their way up the food chain, to produce one pound of tuna. Diatom skeletons fall to the ocean bottom and eventually decay into diatomaceous earth. It is quarried and used in making toothpaste, automobile polish, dynamite, and a variety of other products.

Zooplankton, microscopic animals in the plankton, feed on the phytoplankton. They stay near the bottom during the day, coming to the surface to feed on the plants at night, performing a daily vertical migration that is not fully understood by scientists. The zooplankton become food for larger animals. Their fecal material and remains make up an important part of the substrate—the floors of the oceans and seas—and provide nourishment for bottom feeders.

Various forms of *Radiolaria*, which belong to the zooplankton, are among the most beautiful of sea life, with sculptured skeletons of silica and silica rods radiating out from the body.

Foraminifera, which are related to the amoeba, have most of their bodies covered by shells made of chalk-like calcium carbonate. When they die, their skeletons fall to the sea floor, becoming part of the silt. Their shells make up England's famous White Cliffs of Dover and are used for blackboard chalk. Paleontologists use their ancient remains to date seas, and petroleum companies locate oil deposits with them, giving them their nicknames of "guide fossils" and "oil bugs."

Among the most common and colorful of the protozoa are the dinoflagellates, which share plant and animal characteristics. Ceratium can swim like an animal, but produces its food through photosynthesis in a plant-like manner. It looks a little like a floating anchor, with two flagella for locomotion and a long spine to aid in suspension. It produces its own flickering light, known as bioluminescence, by combining luciferin and oxygen in the presence of the enzyme luciferase.

Noctiluca is a round-shaped dinoflagellate which feeds like an animal on other microscopic organisms. Near its center is a mouth and a tentacle-like structure that helps it catch its prey. It is filled with a greenish gelatinous substance which is lighter than water, making it possible for it to float on the surface. The name *Noctiluca* means "night light," for this bioluminescent protozoan produces some of the brightest lights in the sea. Sparked by darkness and turbulence, they account for the eerie green flashes we sometimes see in the ocean surf at night.

The dinoflagellates *Gonyaulax* and *Gymnodinium* are responsible for the deadly "red tides" that kill fin fish and shellfish along Atlantic and Pacific shores. Six years after a red tide hit, North Carolina's bay scallops are only just beginning to recover.

There are a number of important members of the zooplankton besides the protozoa. Copepods are very small crustaceans with rounded bodies and jointed tails. Their name, which means "oar-footed," comes from the oar-shaped legs with which they propel themselves. It has been suggested that there are more copepods in the world than all other multicellular organisms combined. They feed on the tiny diatoms, sometimes consuming their own weight's worth in a day; in turn, they provide food for invertebrates, fish, birds, and whales.

Many of the organisms that live in the plankton, particularly in coastal areas, are eggs and larvae of more advanced animals. These include the larvae of mollusks, marine worms, crabs, sea stars and most other marine invertebrates. They are only temporary residents, belonging to the Meroplankton, and soon graduate to the larger world visible to human eyes. Their planktonic stages ensure the wide distribution necessary for their continued existence.

While plankton is generally described as being composed of microscopic organisms, there are actually a few organisms, such as the jellyfish and man-o-wars, which grow quite large. Drifting is the main characteristic which defines plankton.

It is easy to forget, when we scan the marshes and sea for birds, fish, and crabs, that the most prolific, and perhaps the most important life, is right under our noses. Hidden by the obscurity of its minuscule size and the limitations of our own imperfect eyesight, a whole world of plants and animals is birthing and dying, pursuing and being pursued, and engaging in a day-to-day struggle for existence. As I returned the water to the sea, one last drop clung to my hand. I gazed at it for a moment, thinking of the poem by William Blake:

> *To see a world in a grain of sand*
> *And a heaven in a wildflower*
>
> *To hold infinity in the palm of your hand*
> *And eternity in an hour*

The Plankton: A World in a Drop of Water

A world, infinite and eternal, clung to my finger for a moment, then fell into the all-engulfing waters of Pamlico Sound.

Death on the Beach

There was no joy to be found on Ocracoke's beach today. The headlines in the newspaper focused on the "Death of Wildlife on the Outer Banks." And when I rode the 17-mile stretch of beach with Bill Caswell, a National Park Service ranger, it was not to enjoy the exquisite panorama of sand and sea I love. It was to look for death.

Bill and I searched the dune line and the ocean shore for victims of the avian cholera epidemic that was decimating the bird population from the Chesapeake Bay to Hatteras. Grimly, we scattered the flocks of gulls gathered at the water's edge, watching for sick or dead birds. Fortunately, at least for today, we found none.

But our relief was offset by the sight of several dolphin carcasses: reminders that six bottlenose dolphins had washed up dead on Ocracoke's beaches in the past two weeks; reminders also of the nine pilot whales that had beached themselves a week earlier at Corolla, 90 miles to the north. At least five of the whales had died.

As we drove along, we listened to a radio transmission from Hatteras Island, where a sick harbor seal had just been found. The report was reminiscent of the young seal we had tried to save just one week before. In spite of all our efforts, the seal, suffering from a deep gash around its neck and respiratory failure, had died before we could get it to a veterinarian.

Before we returned to the village, we stopped to examine the remains of a 15-foot basking shark that had washed up on the beach the day before. The giant beast, a harmless consumer of small fish, made an ugly scar on the pristine sands.

No, we did not find any cholera victims today, but we found nothing to rejoice about on this beautiful March morning. Winter had ravaged aquatic wildlife around the island.

Necropsies, as autopsies on animals are called, were performed on many of the victims found along the beaches. Some of the deaths may have been the result of unusually frigid waters and turbulent storms. Others were likely caused by other natural phenomena. Death, after all, is an integral part of life. But to blame the die-offs on Mother Nature alone is to abdicate our own responsibilities.

There is no doubt that human activities played a role in most of the deaths. These tragedies are signs that our oceans and our earth have reached their capacity for pollution and misuse. The avian cholera that has killed thousands of ducks, loons, and gulls this year was not recorded until the 1930s, and probably was introduced by domestic fowl.

Other die-offs are believed to be the result, at least in part, of stress caused by human activities.

A number of the dolphins, and possibly the basking shark, died in nets pulled by offshore trawlers. This was the probable cause of death as well for several loggerhead sea turtles found on the beach this winter.

The seal deaths that are occurring along the Outer Banks may be the result of pollution, which weakens their immune systems, and starvation due to depleted fisheries, which forces the seals to move south of their traditional ranges. Many show signs of fatal encounters with boats and fish nets.

The people who live at Ocracoke love the ocean and the animals that call it home, as do the tourists who visit the island. But loving them is no longer enough. It is time—past time—for everyone to take his or her part of the responsibility for what is happening and to find out what they can do about it.

I hope that the next time I drive along the beach, it will be to pick up trash, look for turtle tracks, or simply to enjoy its beauty. I hope that the beach will be scattered with scallop and jingle shells instead of dead or dying animals. And I hope that my heart will once again sing with the joy of watching a peach-tinted sunrise, the graceful maneuvers of a formation of pelicans, or the frolics of a pod of playful dolphins.

But I won't forget the warnings of the grim drive I took this morning. Perhaps the tragedies we witnessed this month can become, not harbingers of future death and destruction, but catalysts for a renewed effort to protect the ocean and animals we love.

Palace of Life:
The Oyster

It was one of my favorite places to look for oysters, a winding shallow creek with a soft bottom bordered by marsh cordgrass. Branching off Pamlico Sound, it meandered past juniper trees and wax myrtle shrubs toward the interior of the island. Remote enough to escape the contamination that prevented the harvesting of shellfish in congested areas, it also provided an atmosphere of peace and solitude.

Sometimes, during winter months, I picked up individual oysters as I paddled along, tossed them into the bottom of my boat, and carried them home to steam or fry. But today, I was not looking for dinner. Today, I wanted to share with my friend, Paulette Chitwood, my real fascination with this strange, misshapen creature.

It was not its culinary wonders, exquisite though they are, that intrigued me. Nor its unique life history, nor the important role it plays in purifying the waters of the sound. No, I explained, as I reached into the chill murky water and lifted up a clump of the intertwined mollusks, what most fascinated me was the miniature world contained within and around the calcareous, twisted shells, so complete that an "oyster rock," as a conglomerate of these creatures is called, is classified by scientists as an entire, distinct ecosystem.

Although oysters are creatures of ecological and economic importance, they are best known for their gustatory qualities. They have been enjoyed by such diverse people as prehistoric Indians, ancient Romans, and modern Japanese.

In spite of its unsightly appearance (Robert Hedeen begins his book *The Oyster* with this sage observance: "The oyster is not a beautiful animal, except perhaps to another oyster..."), it has been widely touted in history and literature. William Shakespeare, alluding to its well-known delights, coined the phrase, "the world's mine oyster," back in the sixteenth century. Before that, the Roman philosopher Seneca praised the mollusk, saying, "Oyster...beneficent oyster, all stomachs digest you, all stomachs bless you!" According to Saki (H.H. Munro), the British writer, "oysters are more beautiful than any religion...there's nothing in Christianity or Buddhism that quite matches the selflessness of any oyster."

I can't say I'm such an avid admirer as that, but I have to give the little guys credit for earning such praise. It's certain that oysters have been well-loved by a lot of people. Huge "middens," or garbage heaps, of oyster shells attest to their popularity with early Indian tribes along the Atlantic coast. The Romans engaged in "oyster orgies," and people throughout history have bragged about their abilities to consume oysters in the most disgusting manners. The champion, according to the *Guinness Book of World Records*, is a Marylander known as Tommy "Muskrat" Greene, who, in one minute and 33 seconds, consumed 288 of the luckless creatures!

But, as I explained to Paulette, its place in the dining room is only a small measure of the importance of the oyster. Economically, it has been the basis for the livelihoods and the development of whole communities, particularly on the Chesapeake Bay. Boats such as the skipjack have been designed to harvest it; wars, such as the infamous 200-year "Oyster Wars" between the Virginia and Maryland watermen, have been fought over ownership of its beds.

The Japanese cultivate a small variety of oyster to market as fertilizer. Lime, which is used to improve garden soil, is made from pulverized oyster shells. Farmers add crushed oyster shells to their chicken feed to produce strong egg shells. Even people supplement their calcium, an essential element, by taking pills made of oyster shells. And don't forget that rare and exquisite child of the oyster, beloved of elegant ladies, the pearl.

All of this, however, was probably unbeknownst to the humble oysters, *Crassostrea virginica*, which I now held in my hand. Each individual is a bivalve, a member of the phylum *Mollusca*. Its shell, composed of calcium carbonate, is manufactured by the mantle, which extracts and uses elements from the water.

The outer layer, the periostracum, protects the rest of the shell. The nacreous, or inner layer, reflects light and is often known as mother of pearl. It was used by early Indians as beads and wampum, or money. It is also the nacre from which pearls are formed when deposited around a foreign body lodged in the oyster. (Our Atlantic coast oyster produces, alas, pearls of mediocre quality.)

The oyster itself, thought by some to be a slimy glob, is actually a complex organism, described by T.H. Huxley as "a piece of machinery…greatly more complicated than a watch." It has a three-chambered heart that pumps blue blood (colored by copper instead of iron) through the body. Gills serve not only for respiration, distributing oxygen, but also aid in digestion and the removal of waste. The poor oyster has no brain, merely a pair of ganglia-aggregates of nerve cells that send messages to the rest of the body. For all of its admirable qualities, the oyster is no great thinker.

But what about the notion that the oyster is a great lover, or at least a great inducer of love? Oysters certainly have a varied sex life, since they are hermaphrodites, starting their life as males and two years later changing into females. And they are quite prolific; one female can produce 500 million eggs in one year. Whether there is any truth, however, to the belief that the oyster is an aphrodisiac is uncertain. Some scientists speculate that zinc, necessary for male reproductive activity and contained in high quantities in oysters, is the answer. Galen, the Greek physician living in the second century, believed in it, at any rate, and prescribed oysters for sexual problems.

Like many bivalves, the oyster is a filter, or ciliary, feeder, and through this function, it provides one of its greatest services. It draws water into its system and filters out plankton, which it ingests by means of tiny tentacles, called cilia, along its mantle. In the process, it filters silt, trash, and pollutants out of the water, thus cleansing it. It is said that one oyster will filter 50 gallons of water on a warm day.

In cleansing the water around it, however, it absorbs pollutants. For this reason, many oyster beds, as well as other shellfish areas, have been closed. Contaminated shellfish can cause hepatitis and other serious illnesses. That is why I chose this remote, unpopulated creek to gather my oysters.

Oysters have to contend with more than just pollution. From the moment they are expelled from the female as eggs and fertilized by the male sperm, they lead a dangerous existence. Their first days are spent as free-swimming larvae known as trochophores, then as veligers, before metamorphosing into tiny specks known as spat. These spat attach themselves to a solid object, often another oyster, and settle down to spend the rest of their lives as stationary organisms. But of the enormous number of eggs hatched in a season by a female, perhaps only a dozen survive.

For those survivors, life holds many threats, including hungry predators (such as starfish and skates), internal parasites (such as flatworms), diseases (such as MSX and Dermo), suffocation by siltation (often caused by such human activities as plowing fields or construction), and, of course, predation (known as harvesting) by humans.

All of which made the little ecosystem I held in my hand more precious and intriguing. This conglomerate of oysters provided shelter, homes, and restaurant service for a variety of different animals. Scientist H. W. Wells estimated in 1961 that as many as 300 species, representing most of the phyla, may inhabit a good-sized oyster bar.

Sponges, anemones, and sea squirts cling to the outside of the shells, as do barnacles and several kinds of mollusks. Algae and plant-like Bryozoans grow on the rugged surfaces. Oyster or pea crabs

make their homes inside the oyster shells. At least five kinds of segmented worms work their way through the jungle gym of oyster
shells, and limey tube worms leave their tube-like casings on the surface. Young blue crabs scurry along the bottom, and small fish drift
through the calcareous crevices. Larger predators hover at the out-
skirts, searching for prey.

Most of these animals practice commensalism, benefiting from the
oysters without harming them. Others, such as the flatworms, are
parasites. Their presence causes harm, though usually not death, to
their hosts. Still other oyster bar inhabitants prey on the oysters. Sea
stars pry open the two valves and devour the live mollusks.
Gastropods, such as the oyster drill, secrete a softening agent, which
allows them to pierce the oyster's shell and consume it. Jellyfish,
skates, and bony fish eat the eggs and larvae of oysters. They themselves are preyed upon by larger predators, all forming a part of the
food chain in the oyster bar ecosystem.

Paulette and I counted nine different animals in the clump I held
in my hand, including ribbed mussels, slipper shells, snail fur, and
tube worm casings. We pretended it was a miniature castle, with its
residents carrying on the business of a kingdom, each worker and
each task essential to its welfare. Indeed, each organism in my hand
was important to the welfare of the creek, the sound, and the earth
itself.

I carefully replaced the oyster rock in the creek where I had found it. As a delicious dinner and appetizer, a unique organism, and a whole ecosystem, the oyster is a wonderful creature. Cyrano de Bergerac, the seventeenth century French writer with the famous nose, summarized the importance of the oyster in these words: "You have never seen the sea but in an oyster on the shell."

A Legacy from the Past: Whales

Even from a distance, I could see that the object lying on the beach was unusual. I was driving along the ocean shore, picking up bottles, plastic bags, and other trash, and tossing them into the bed of the National Park Service truck I was using. This object was no piece of trash, however.

I stopped the truck, slipped it into neutral, and got out to look. The object was round, about 12 inches across, with two wing-like projections extending out another eight inches on each side. It was rough and worn, gray with age, and as I found when I lifted it, quite heavy. I am not an expert on anatomy, but it was easy to see that it was a vertebra.

From its condition, I knew that it was very, very old; from its size, I had no doubt that it came from a whale.

The truck was not due back for several hours, so I was in no hurry. I sat down in the cool sand next to the whale bone, rubbing my finger gently along its surface as I studied it. I tried to imagine the giant creature it had once belonged to.

I pretended for a moment that the vertebra had been part of an ancient *Archaeoceti*, living 45 to 50 million years ago during the Eocene Period. Thought by many scientists to be the ancestor of modern whales, it would only recently (geologically speaking) have returned to the sea from whence it had sprung.

No one knows why, but long ago, for some reason—perhaps to escape predators or insects, or to find food—a small mammal, after making all the necessary adaptations to live on land, deserted it. It became streamlined for travel in the water, and its breathing apparatus migrated to the top, forming one or two blowholes. Its front legs evolved into fish-like fins known as flippers, and its back legs disappeared. Its tail changed to resemble that of a fish, except that the flukes grew horizontally instead of vertically, giving it an up-and-down motion when it swam. It produced a heavy layer of blubber to protect it against the frigid temperatures of the north seas.

In spite of all this, however, it remained a mammal—with lungs instead of gills, warm-blooded instead of cold-blooded, giving birth to live young and producing milk, gradually making adaptations to survive in a liquid environment. *Archaeoceti*, my imaginary whale, had not perfected these adaptations and eventually became extinct.

Its descendants, or perhaps their cousins, continued to evolve, however, becoming the animals scientists call cetaceans (from the Greek and Latin words for whale). By the late Miocene Period, 10

to 12 million years ago, they had branched off into two different suborders: the *Mysticeti*, or "mustached" whales, and the *Odontoceti*, or "toothed" whales. The *Mysticeti* include the baleen whales such as the humpbacks, blues, and rights. The *Odontoceti* include the orcas, sperm whales, dolphins, and porpoises. All of these migrate along the coast of North Carolina.

Now I pictured my imaginary cetacean as a young right whale traveling north along the Carolina coast, gulping down huge mouthfuls of its favorite food, copepod stew, and conversing with its fellow whales in a series of moans. It might have slapped its flippers as it played with other young members of the pod.

Eubalaena glacialis, the northern right whale, was once common along this coastline. Right whales are large baleen whales, up to 50 feet in length and 100 tons in weight, with an original range that spanned both hemispheres and oceans. They derive their name from the Greek word for "right" and the Latin for "whale." Those that live in the northern hemisphere, such as this one would have, are identified by the Greek word for "icy" or "frozen."

Right whales have large heads with crusty, horny outgrowths called callosities. The largest of these, located in front of the two blowholes, is known as the "bonnet." Whale lice live on the callosities, giving them a yellow, pink, white, or orange appearance. They have large broad flippers, deeply notched flukes, and no dorsal fin. They are easily identified by their blows, which create a V-shaped fountain of spray.

These whales are slow swimmers and do not engage in long migrations, as do many of the cetaceans. Quite acrobatic for their size, they engage in flipper-slapping, breaching, and sometimes "head-standing." They used to be found in large herds of around a hundred, but today, it is rare to see even a dozen. They communicate through a variety of moans believed to be produced by forcing air through their blowholes.

Mating usually occurs in winter or spring, and males often fight over the females. Birthing takes place at the same time of year, with the calf emerging tail-first. Either the mother or attending whales immediately help the newborn calf to the surface to get its first breath. For the first few months after birthing, mothers and calves remain isolated in "nurseries," but later rejoin the main pod.

Right whales seem to have a distinct preference for the tiny crustaceans in the plankton known as copepods. They open their wide mouths and take in great mouthfuls of water, straining out the copepods with hair-like strands of baleen and expelling the left-over water through the sides of their mouths.

The right whale received its name because it was the "right" whale for whalers to hunt and kill. It was slow, easy to catch, and relatively docile. Its blubber produced oil of the highest quality, which was used as fuel for lighting and heating, and its enormous head contained large supplies of baleen, or whalebone, which was all the rage for women's corsets in the nineteenth century. They were slaughtered by the hundreds in early centuries, and by the thousands when modern whaling equipment became available.

North Carolina used to have the largest whaling industry south of New Jersey, with whalers operating out of Shackleford and Bogue Banks and, to some extent, Ocracoke and Hatteras Islands. Much of the whaling centered on "drift" whales, which washed up on the beaches, but documents indicate that whaling expeditions began targeting whales off the coast of North Carolina in the 1660s.

According to records from the early 1700s, eight or nine whales were taken in one year by two boats operating out of Ocracoke. The main target of these hunts was the friendly, docile right whale.

Perhaps my imaginary whale had met its death not far from where I now stood. It might have spied a boat and, with a number of its companions, decided to escort it for a ways on its voyage. Perhaps it chose the wrong vessel—a whaling ship—and found that its playful greetings were returned by shouting men with harpoons.

It would have been a sad tale. But the story of the hunting of right whales is just that. These once bountiful, playful, and intelligent creatures have been hunted to the point of extinction. There are only an estimated 300 northern right whales left, and in spite of international laws that protect them, it is uncertain whether they can recover. But I was only dreaming. I would never know the history of the vertebra I had found, or what kind of whale it had belonged to. When I returned, I would give it to the National Park Service rangers at the Visitors Center, and perhaps they could use it to teach visitors at Ocracoke more about these great cetaceans. Perhaps that teaching would play some small role in helping to protect our oceans' remaining whales so that they could continue to live and multiply. Perhaps one day in the future, northern right whales, similar to the one I had imagined, would be the "right" whales to see tail-lobbing and frolicking in great herds in the waters of North Carolina.

Aftermath of a Storm

Wrapped in blankets, I write by kerosene lantern. We are still having power outages two days after the March tempest that some people are calling the "storm of the century."

According to my schedule, I should be tutoring now, and in a little while I would be turning on the Moody Blues concert on PBS. Instead, I sit contemplating the fury and power of nature, which has tossed the schedules and plans of half of the country into the wind.

As inconvenient as it is, this electric outage is a mere annoyance in the chaos wrought by the storm. Yesterday, driving down the beach from Nags Head, I saw overturned vans, shutters ripped from houses, boats tossed pell-mell from their docks. And on television, I learned about lost homes and violent deaths, all vestiges of the storm.

But now my mind dwells on another aspect of the storm. Earlier today, I saw what nature could do to nature, and in a way, it is even more disquieting. I went out with two friends, Mickey Baker and Carmie Prete, on what might be described as a shell-collecting orgy.

Many times, I have walked the beach searching for shells and other treasures that the ocean might have tossed ashore. With luck, I might find a few scotch bonnets or an olive shell.

But today!

Today, the ocean seemed to have gone mad, spewing onto the beach the contents of a gargantuan feast. The sand was littered—no, piled—with the skeletons and bodies of the myriad creatures that inhabit the sea.

Sea stars were strewn everywhere, and at the ocean's edge, their corpses were piled several inches high. The shells of mollusks and bivalves were scattered far up the beach to the flood line. There were colorful scallops and cockles, whelks of every size and hue, moonshells, olive shells, and scotch bonnets. Great masses of seaweed lay tangled with the remains of sea cucumbers, sea squirts, and jellyfish. I wished that I could find a pen shell, and there at my feet was a magnificent specimen eight inches long. It was, as Carmie remarked, like Christmas morning for a shell collector.

I was awed by the quantity and variety of the now-stilled life lying around me. A number of these creatures were unknown to me, in spite of the many hours I had spent driving and walking this beach. What mystery must still lie hidden beneath those dark waters, secrets not only of the present, but of the distant past.

Many of the shells we found after the storm showed signs that they had been recently alive. Some were ripped out of the Gulf Stream by currents driven by violent winds. Others, like the voracious lobed moonshells, were dislodged from shallow, off-shore waters, rudely interrupted as they feasted on unfortunate surf clams. Their natural colors were still vibrant, the swirls and ridges in their calcareous exoskeletons still crisp and perfect.

But scientists, using radiocarbon-dating techniques, have discovered that most of the seashells found along Atlantic beaches are several thousand years old. The whelk shell I had picked up, blackened by a natural manganese stain, might have been alive in the days of the Early Woodland Indians. It might have washed ashore in another big storm and been picked up by other hands. Perhaps, long ago, an Indian child held it against her ear and listened to the sea.

The weathered oyster shells that lay interspersed in the melee were proof that Ocracoke, like other barrier islands, was slowly moving westward toward the mainland. These ugly but succulent bivalves had lived in ancient oyster beds near this very spot. Only then, this spot was soundside, not oceanside. Gradually, over the centuries, the island had eroded and shifted westward, leaving these oyster shell relics behind to remind us of the transiency of existence.

Some of the shells at my feet were even older. New, more sophisticated amino-acid–dating techniques are proving that many of the very weathered, discolored shells and shell fragments on the beach date back to the Pleistocene, known as the Ice Age, which lasted from approximately two million to ten thousand years ago. These blackened quahogs, or hard-shelled clams, may have siphoned plankton and water through their partially opened shells as mammoths and saber-toothed tigers stalked the marshes.

Some day soon, I'll walk out on the beach again. The sands will be clean and white, with only an occasional scallop shell and a few coquinas disturbing the surface. The sea will lie quiet and peaceful, betraying no sign of the millions of creatures engaged in life and death struggles within its dark recesses. But I will know, remembering this day, how frightening the ocean can be, and I will dream of other days when winds and currents will tear through it again, revealing its magnificent mysteries.

Spring

The Ocracoke Ponies: Wild No More

Bonita Sorpresa! A pretty surprise!

That's what Ranger Bill Caswell had when he went to the pony pens one Saturday morning in March. The ponies looked fine, but there was something different in the pasture. For a moment he thought it was a deer, but soon there was no doubt. The Ocracoke pony herd had a new foal.

The year before, the veterinarian from Hatteras had diagnosed Jim, the beautiful, 25-year-old Banker stallion, with cancer. In an effort to preserve his original Spanish bloodline before he died, National Park Service rangers tried to breed him with two of the Ocracoke mares, Nevada and Lindessa. But they knew that because of his illness, it might not work. And sure enough, the pregnancy tests for both mares came back negative. It looked as if there would be no new ponies this year.

So the little chestnut filly cavorting in the field was a complete surprise. I stopped by the pony pens that morning, and Bill pointed her out in excitement. She was a beauty. Bill brought her and her mother, Nevada, in from the pasture and gave them a private corral and stable. People came from the village to admire the new foal, and she put on a good show, running and bucking and butting her mother. In no time, she was a pet, following the park rangers and volunteers who took care of her.

But she didn't have a name. It was Howard Bennink, a teacher at Ocracoke School and a part-time ranger, who came up with the idea. Why not have a contest at the school, letting the students pick out a name? It was agreed, and all kinds of names came pouring in. It was hard to choose among all the selections, but the final vote was for "Bonita Sorpresa," which is Spanish for "Pretty Surprise." For that's what the little filly was.

The wild ponies of Ocracoke live today in a 180-acre pen that adjoins Pamlico Sound and includes salt marshes, woods, and meadowlands. There are 25 ponies, including the new foal. The herd is managed by the National Park Service, which provides veterinary care, shelter, and supplemental feed.

But not so very long ago, the ponies ran free on the island. Legend has it that they arrived on the Outer Banks in the sixteenth century, brought over on Spanish ships. The ships may have wrecked on the treacherous off-shore shoals, allowing the ponies to escape, or the Spaniards may have deliberately released them as they prepared to return to Spain.

Another theory is that Sir Richard Grenville, leading an expedition from England in 1580, stopped at a Spanish island to pick up supplies and stock (including some of the Spanish ponies) on his way to Roanoke Island in North Carolina. His ship ran aground at Ocracoke Inlet and some of the ponies were released to lighten the load so the ship could break free.

However they may have gotten here, there is little doubt that they are of Spanish origin. They still have the characteristics of the small, hardy horses bred by the Moors, combining their Iberian stock with North African Barbs and Arabians. They are really small horses rather than ponies, with short backs (having one fewer lumbar vertebra than other horses), short legs, and a sloping croup. They are even-tempered, intelligent, and tough.

When Ocracoke was settled by the English, they began riding the ponies and using them for plowing gardens, pulling carts, and hauling freight. When the Life Saving Service, forerunner of the Coast

Guard, was established in the nineteenth century, the Ocracoke ponies were used for patrolling the beaches and rescuing shipwreck victims. The main herds, however, continued to run free.

There was a round-up, or pony-penning, every year on the Fourth of July. Islanders would start at the far end of the island, on horseback, herding the bands of ponies toward the village. There would be several hundred horses, and as the stallions from the various bands were bunched together, they would fight. People from the village would gather around to watch, and there was a festive air on the island, with lemonade, ice cream, and other treats.

Several areas were used, over the years, for penning the ponies. One was in front of the Island Inn, one at Windmill Point, one near Sam Jones' Castle, and one at the cowpens (the present-day pony pen.) There, the ponies were branded, gelded, and broken. Some were separated to be used in the village or sold on the mainland, and the rest were turned loose to run free again.

During the 1950s, Captain Marvin Howard, retired from the U.S. Army Corps of Engineers, turned Ocracoke's Boy Scouts into the only mounted scout troop in the country. Those boys who did not already have ponies caught and broke one, and they all learned to ride in formation. A number of native Ocracokers today have fond memories of their scouting days, when they went on camping trips, rode in parades, and entered races at the Pirates' Jamboree in Buxton.

But the carefree days of the wild-roaming ponies were numbered. An epidemic of blind staggers killed many of the village mounts. When Highway 12 was built, it became unsafe for the ponies to run free. The Park Service, which was in charge of the recently established Cape Hatteras National Seashore, began enforcing a ban on free grazing, forcing the islanders to either fence or sell the ponies. The Park Service agreed to let the Boy Scouts build a pen for the remaining unclaimed ponies, and issued them a special use permit. The community and the state pitched in to help cover the cost of maintaining the herd.

In the mid-1960s, however, the Boy Scouts had to give up keeping the herd, and the fate of the Ocracoke ponies was left in jeopardy. The U.S. government did not want to assume responsibility, maintaining that the ponies were not a natural resource. But in response to public sentiment they agreed, in 1967, to take over their care as a cultural resource. By then, the herd was reduced to only 19 ponies, and it continued to decline until it reached an all-time low of nine ponies in 1976.

Since then, the Park Service rangers have worked hard to build up the herd. They bred some of the mares to an Andalusian stallion, whose bloodline closely resembled that of the original Banker ponies. With the help of volunteers, they have trained several of the ponies to use for beach patrol, and they ride them in the Fourth of July parade.

Meanwhile, life continues for the ponies, in many ways similar to the way it always was. They still roam through the salt marsh, eating the marsh grass, seeking shade and shelter in the juniper trees, wading into the waters of the sound to escape the insects, birthing and dying. But they do it within the confines of a fence.

Not long before the birth of the little filly, the village was saddened by the death of Dusky, one of the oldest ponies in the herd, and one of the last to have roamed truly free. But just as springtime brings new life to the trees and the flowers, it brought new life to the Ocracoke pony herd. The birth of Bonita Sorpresa assured that the Spanish bloodline of the first ponies to come to Ocracoke hundreds of years ago will continue.

Ocracoke's famous wild ponies are wild no longer. But were they ever truly wild? And do they really belong on the island?

For centuries, they roamed free, living off the tough marsh grasses, adjusting to drinking the brackish water, learning to evade the ravenous insects. They made their own place on the island, often with no help or interference from humans. They not only survived, but they also thrived, becoming a part of the ecosystem.

But they were nonetheless transplants, brought from another continent. They were domestic animals, running wild. In becoming a part of the island ecosystem, they pushed natural organisms aside, permanently altering Ocracoke's environment.

On the Outer Banks, as in many other places, scientists, public officials, and concerned citizens argue whether transplanted and feral animals have a place in our natural world. The question is a difficult one. It involves ethical and emotional issues on many levels and in many places.

What about the ponies still running free at Assateague Island and Corolla? The romanticized wild horses that roam the prairies of the west?

What about the feral house cats that roam free on Ocracoke and many other places?

The issue involves wild animals and plants that were brought in from other countries: starlings, English sparrows, nutria, kudzu.

What about wild animals such as the cattle egret, coyote, and brown-headed cowbird, which moved to new territory on their own? What about harbor seals and brown pelicans, which are even now expanding their ranges along the Atlantic Seaboard?

Are the wild ponies of Ocracoke a part of the lore of the wildness of the island? Or are they part of the story of how humans have altered and impacted it?

Whatever the answer, there are few things more beautiful to me than the sight of a band of ponies silhouetted against the sea, tossing their heads and thundering through the surf.

Searching for Piping Plovers

"We need someone to check on the piping plovers," Wayne Elliot, a ranger, told me when I stopped at the National Park Service office.

I was helping with the shorebird research project the Park Service was conducting. So I climbed in the four-wheel-drive pickup truck, picked up a friend who wanted to help, and drove down the airport ramp to the beach. At this time of year, late March, it was practically deserted. I headed toward South Point.

The tide was going out, leaving the beach strewn with the shells. A line of pelicans soared single-file above the ocean, watching the water below for signs of fish. Herring gulls stood in small groups close to the dunes, and an occasional willet waded in the surf. But we saw no signs of piping plovers, so I turned the truck around and headed toward the other end of the island.

As I drove, I explained to my friend that the small shorebird we were looking for was protected under the Endangered Species Act as a threatened species. It had been hunted in the late 1800s and early 1900s to the point of extinction, along with a number of other water birds. In 1918, the Migratory Bird Act halted the killing, and the piping plovers made a gradual recovery until around 1940.

Since then, however, many birds, including the piping plovers, had been declining again. This time the culprit was not hunting but loss of habitat.

As beaches are developed along the Atlantic coast, shore birds are left with no place to rest, feed, or raise their young. They are shy birds and do not like to nest in areas where there is human traffic. Their eggs, laid in shallow pockets in the sand, blend with the pebbles and shells and are often driven over or stepped on. Dogs chase the adults and disturb the nests. Sea gulls, more numerous than ever today, eat the eggs and the nestlings. Feral cats, and in some areas, raccoons, prey on the nests.

This was the reason we were now driving along the beach, trying to locate nesting pairs. The park rangers would rope off prospective nesting areas so that they would not be disturbed. As we headed up the beach, we sighted a pod of bottlenose dolphins frolicking in the surf. Just as the birds migrated north for the summer, so did these friendly marine mammals. Small flocks of sanderlings, known locally as beachbirds, darted in and out of the waves as we drove by. But we saw no piping plovers.

As we passed the ramp near the pony pens, we saw flashes of silver and bursts of sea spray out beyond the surf, sure signs of jumping fish—sea mullet, perhaps, trying to escape a school of blues. Several pairs of oystercatchers searched along the shore, picking at choice tidbits in the sand, looking clownish in their striking black and white plumage with their bright orange beaks and eyes. They were just returning from a winter spent in South America. But we still saw no piping plovers.

We were nearing the north end of the beach when something caught my eye, a little flurry of motion out on the waves' edge. My mind clicked and I slowly backed up to look again. Two small birds were running back and forth along the surf, pecking at worms, crustaceans, and other tiny creatures. They were about seven inches long, sand-colored with white undersides and black collars around their necks. Yes, they were plovers, all right.

I took out my binoculars and studied them more closely. They had black bars across their foreheads, orange legs, and black-tipped, orange beaks. There was no doubt now—we had located a pair of piping plovers.

They kept their distance from the truck, but continued to search for food, probing into the sand. Because their beaks are shorter than those of most shorebirds, they cannot reach down far, but mostly feed close to the surface. We could hear their melodic, piping cries as they paused now and then, bobbing up and down at the water's edge.

This was the time of year for the birds to be migrating north. North Carolina is the southernmost part of their nesting range, so only a few pairs were expected to stop and nest here. Others would follow the coast north as far as Canada. Those that stayed would begin sitting on nests in late April and early May. They would lay four finely speckled, light gray-brown eggs which would hatch in about thirty days. Both parents would attend the nest, feigning broken wings to lead intruders away.

The hatchlings are precocious, which means that they can follow their parents and feed themselves soon after emerging from the eggs. They reach fledgling age in about a month and are ready to join the adult plovers in the fall when they migrate south, some as far as Mexico. A few spend the winter at Ocracoke and adjoining islands.

My friend and I were thrilled at the opportunity to watch these exquisite shore birds, but we felt sad as well. I imagined what it was like 200 years ago, when plovers, sandpipers, and other shore birds blackened the skies during migration time.

I wondered what it would be like in another 20 years. Would our children have to visit a zoo or look at a book to see these birds?

Although piping plovers are the only shore birds frequenting this seashore that are on the endangered species list, all such birds are in trouble. They face the same habitat destruction and disturbances that threaten the little plover.

By locating the nesting area so that it could be set aside for the summer, my friend and I could play only a small role in helping them. But we hoped that this study, along with other efforts nation-wide, would find solutions that would protect these and other species of shore birds. We hoped that our grandchildren would experience the same thrill we did as we watched them dashing through the surf, bobbing up and down, piping their melodic songs of joy.

A Welcome Visit in the Night: Frogs and Toads

It was a miserable night to be out, drizzly wet and just cold enough to cut through your sweatshirt and jeans and give you a thorough chill. There were puddles in the low spots of the yard that would seep right through your shoes if you accidentally blundered into one.

I was just arriving home from a trip up the beach and was weaving my way around the puddles toward the house when a sudden movement brought me up short. Then there it was again, on the ground in front of the porch. Another look sent a thrill of joy through me. It was a toad!

It took another hop, probably disgruntled at being disturbed on this magnificent evening, for it was indeed great weather for a toad. I stayed for a moment and watched it, fond memories running through my head. There was a time when toads and frogs were among my favorite playmates. Spring wasn't spring without a goldfish bowl full of tadpoles to watch grow into frogs. And summer wasn't summer without the deep hoarse bellow of a bullfrog and a musical chorus of peepers.

But I hadn't seen a toad or a frog for a while, and this one was a welcome visitor at my doorstep. I admonished it to watch out for the orange tomcat I had seen as I pulled into the driveway, and I hurried up the steps into my house and out of the rain.

Later that evening, as I lay soaking in the bathtub with a glass of wine, I thought about my little visitor. Of course, I reminded myself, it was not really a visitor; this was its yard (or at least its family's yard) long before I arrived. But now I rarely see one—so seldom, indeed, that I felt as if I should have rolled out a red carpet for this one.

Amphibians have always been scarce on Ocracoke. There are no documented accounts of salamanders and only four recorded species of frogs and toads. This is because of the scarcity of fresh water and the large amount of salt spray which, during storms, reaches almost all areas of the island. Amphibians have moist, sensitive skin which absorbs the salt, resulting sometimes in their death. Those that do live

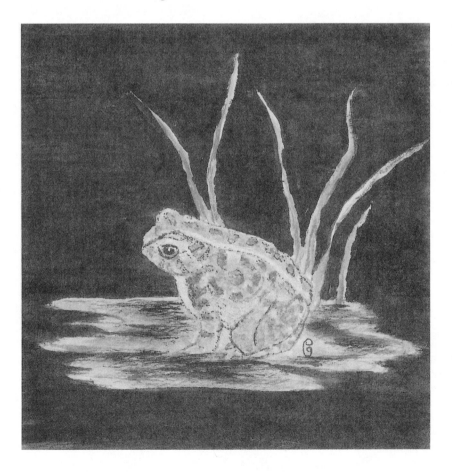

on Ocracoke are especially salt-tolerant and traditionally do quite well here.

Both toads and frogs have short backs, webbed feet, large eyes, excellent hearing, and highly developed vocal chords which are used during mating. They lay their eggs in fresh water, and these eggs hatch into unique, gilled larvae called tadpoles or polliwogs. Toads normally have drier, bumpier skin and shorter legs and spend more time on land than frogs. Ocracoke has resident populations of Fowler's toads, southern leopard frogs, green tree frogs, and their close cousins, the squirrel tree frogs.

My visitor no doubt was a Fowler's toad (*Bufo woodhousei*). Two to three inches long, it is gray, olive, or brown with a light stripe down its back and numerous dark dorsal spots containing three or more small warts. Fowler's toads breed on Ocracoke from March to May, and females lay two long strings of about 3,500 eggs each. The eggs hatch into tadpoles or polliwogs in about a week, and develop into adult toads one to two months later. They can live for up to 15 years. They hibernate in the winter by digging into the mud or finding a safe spot under a log, and males greet the spring with loud discordant rasping calls which last up to four seconds.

Leopard frogs, so named because of the large distinct spots which adorn their green or brown bodies, are about the same size as Fowler's toads. They breed in winter and early spring and occasionally in the fall, producing a series of guttural croaks and clucks.

Ocracoke's two species of tree frogs, the green and the squirrel, are easily confused. The green frog is larger, growing up to two and a half inches, and is always the same bright yellow-green. Its mating call is bell-like, a high nasal sound repeated once a second. The squirrel frog seldom exceeds an inch and a half, and can change from solid bright green to spotted dull brown. Its voice resembles that of a chattering squirrel, which is where it gets its name.

Both come out of hiding at night and are often seen near lights, where their insect dinners congregate. They are excellent climbers and are likely to be found not only in trees, but also on windows and glass doors. One resident of Ocracoke told me that when she checked her birdhouse looking for baby birds, she found instead that it was full of tree frogs.

I am not the only one to notice that there are fewer frogs and toads at Ocracoke, or indeed, anywhere. Scientists world-wide are concerned about the disappearance of amphibians and have offered various explanations. Destruction of habitat certainly plays an important role, as does air pollution and the extensive use of pesticides. Cats and dogs kill frogs and toads in suburban areas, and automobiles crush innumerable ones when summer showers draw them onto the roads to hunt insects. Acid rain, caused by automobile and power plant emissions containing sulfur dioxin and nitrous oxide, create spawning pools too acidic for tadpoles to survive in.

But frogs and their cousins seem to be also disappearing in areas where none of these things is taking place. Many scientists believe that they are dying as a result of ultraviolet rays entering the atmosphere through a "hole" in the ozone layer caused by man-made CFCs (chlorofluorocarbons). Amphibians, because of their sensitive, highly absorbent skins, are more vulnerable to these rays than other animals.

No one is certain if these are the reasons we are seeing fewer frogs and toads at Ocracoke. It could simply be a result of several dry seasons or unusually high levels of salt in their spawning waters. We do know, however, that much of the frog-supporting habitat on the island is being destroyed and that there is periodic spraying for mosquitoes in the summer, when frogs are feeding on insects. We know that there are lots of cats wandering in the night, searching for something to eat. And more cars are on the roads here than ever before. We also know that ultraviolet radiation is enough of a danger for warnings to be issued on the radio.

When I was a kid living in Virginia, I had a self-imposed mission every spring. All kinds of frogs and toads would lay eggs in my father's swimming pool, and these eggs would hatch into thousands of tadpoles. When it was time for my father to empty the pool for painting, my best friend and I would spend days carrying tadpoles in buckets to the pond across the road. As the deadline for painting approached, I would plead with my father to wait another day, and I could sometimes even coax him into helping. Somehow, we always managed to rescue the whole poolful.

How I wish that things were that easy today. Was the world that much simpler back then, or was it my childlike perception that made it appear so? By the time our task was completed, I felt that we had rescued the world and made it safe for polliwogs and frogs.

I know better now. The dangers faced by the world's amphibians and other wild creatures today are complex and widespread, and there are no simple solutions.

I hope that the next rainy summer day on Ocracoke will bring with it a symphony of trills, peeps, and croaks, that my windowpane will be a mess of froggy footprints, and that I will have to dodge numerous disgruntled toads when I approach my house. But I am worried that this will not be so, and my joy at greeting Mr. Toad on this rainy night is tempered with sadness.

Spirit Bird of Ocracoke: The Loon

If you have ever heard the wild, unearthly cry of a Common Loon, you'll probably never forget it. The call of the loon has long been considered a symbol of the American wilderness, particularly of the far northern lakes where they spend their summers.

While most people are familiar with the loon in its summer range, few realize that loons spend their winters in the southeast, swimming and diving along the cold, dark waters of the Atlantic shoreline.

Dressed in soft grays and browns, they moult during February and March to grow the striking black-and-white plumage of their better-known summer attire. By June, most of them have flown north to their breeding grounds, but juveniles and a few adults remain through the summer.

I well remember my first encounter with a loon at Ocracoke. I was kayaking in the Pamlico Sound one late spring afternoon, watching the colors of the sky change from blue-gray to red and gold, listening to that special silence that precedes sunset on the sound. I heard a soft, melodious cry, not far away. Although I had not heard the sound before and did not then realize that loons frequented this area, I immediately thought, *A loon!*

Sure enough, as I slowed my paddle and gazed around me, I saw the sleek, black-and-white form of this legendary bird surface in front of me. I glimpsed it for a moment; then it was gone, diving under the dark, gently rolling waters of the estuary.

Soon I heard the cry again, this time to my right, and there was the loon again. I was haunted by its soft musical wail every few minutes as I paddled my kayak toward shore. I have been haunted by it ever since.

The term "common" is misleading for the loon, for there is nothing common about "*Gavia immer*," as it is known to scientists. Loons are the oldest birds in North America. They have lived here, following the same annual rhythms, for 60 million years. Formerly called "great northern divers," they are great swimmers and divers, able to stay underwater for more than a minute, shooting rapidly to great depths in pursuit of the fish they eat. They are aided by their solid bones, making them extremely heavy compared to other birds, whose bones are hollow.

The loon is strictly a water bird, and a healthy one is seldom seen on shore except to nest. Its webbed feet are placed far back under its

belly, which helps in swimming and diving but makes walking on land impossible. On the few occasions when a loon finds itself out of the water, it must scoot along on its belly in little leaps. It cannot take off and fly from the land, and has difficulty launching from the water; but once in flight, it is swift and strong.

There is certainly nothing common about the language of loons. They have four distinct cries. The "tremolo," used during breeding and nesting, sounds like maniacal human laughter and is the basis for the expression "crazy as a loon." Adult loons talk to their chicks in the soft cooing tones known as "hoots." Each male loon has its own individual version of the "yodel," a song used for identification among themselves (also used by scientists to distinguish birds). The eerie "wail" was believed to be an omen of death among the early Chippewa Indians.

Loons are devoted mates and parents. There is evidence that most of them mate for life, spending winters alone in the Atlantic but reuniting each spring on the northern lakes. There, the males perform dramatic courtship displays, rearing up out of the water with their wings spread. After mating, they build a shallow nest and take turns sitting on two eggs. After the eggs hatch, the parents carry the chicks on their backs until they are old enough to swim.

The young feed on small fish and crustaceans through the summer, growing and gaining strength until, at 11 weeks of age, they are ready to fly. In late summer, the parents head south, leaving the fledgling loons on their own.

Soon, instinct draws the fledglings to congregate with other young loons, and in early fall they begin their own journey south. Traveling alone or in small groups, they stop at the Chesapeake Bay to feed on menhaden and other fish, then proceed on to the wintering grounds. Here, the young loons will spend the next three years, not flying north again until fully mature.

Loons are not common in terms of their abundance, either. Most Americans will never have a chance to see or hear one of these birds. As the wilderness declines, so do these ancient denizens of the wild.

Old-timers on Ocracoke say they used to see scores of them off the coast, but not today. Scientists link their dramatic decline to a number of factors. Hunting, illegal now, wiped out large numbers of loons, even though loon is not considered a choice meat. (Being called a "loon-eater" used to be considered an insult in eastern North Carolina. I know someone who nearly got punched out for saying it.)

In the loon's northern range, vacation homes and other development on the lakes reduce nesting sites, and boaters unintentionally frighten loons off nests. Recent studies have shown that lead poisoning from the ingestion of fishing sinkers has a significant impact on loon populations. Many northern lakes where loons nest have become contaminated by acid rain from automobile exhaust and factory emissions. Loon chicks, unable to find enough to eat in these sterile lakes, starve to death.

On their winter range, loons sometimes follow fish into gill nets, becoming entangled and drowning. I remember my second encounter with a loon at Ocracoke. It was not as happy as the first. A fisherman brought over a young loon he had found in his net, still alive. It was hypothermic from being trapped in the ice-cold water and had inhaled water into its lungs. It died within a few hours.

That was the first of many loons I have tried to save since coming to the island. I have worked with many birds, but none has puzzled or intrigued me as much as this beautiful, high-spirited diver with its plaintive voice. Many loons beach themselves without visible signs of injury, and are too weak and disoriented to return to the sea when we find them. Others, unfortunately, are already dead.

Biologists are puzzled about what is causing them to weaken and die. One theory is that they are being poisoned by mercury ingested in the north, where the acid rain has leached this deadly metal into the lakes. Another is that they are starving to death as a result of depleted fish stocks or altered migration patterns of their food fish. Disease, pollution, or some other mysterious killer may be to blame.

Many concerned people are trying to understand and protect the loon. For those of us who love wild places, whether a far northern lake or the ocean off North Carolina, this mysterious bird is a symbol. The Cree Indians believed the loon to be the spirit of a warrior denied entrance into heaven.

To me, the loon is the spirit of freedom and wilderness.

The Pleasant Plain:
Ocracoke's Salt Marshes

How ample, the marsh and the sea and the sky!
A league and a league of marsh grass, waist high,
Broad in the blade, green, and all of a height
And unflicked with a light or a shade
Stretch leisurely off, in a pleasant plain
To the terminal blue of the main.

Ye marshes, how candid and simple
and nothing-withholding and free
Ye publish yourselves to the sky
And offer yourselves to the sea!

Sidney Lanier's haunting poem, "The Marshes of Glynn," comes to mind as I gaze along the meandering shoreline of Pamlico Sound. I am sitting on a twisted piece of driftwood, washed in by the last storm. A blanket of wheat-colored marsh grass lies at my back, a carpet of sun-dried, black eel grass at my feet. I sought peace and quiet when I trudged down the sandy path leading to this isolated retreat, and I have found it.

Ocracoke's salt marshes hold a special allure for me. Whereas the ocean awes me with its power and sense of eternity, the soundside of the island charms me with its friendliness and feeling of security. On a day like this, when the breeze coming over the water is gentle and the skies are a soft blue-gray, I feel that I can sit here until I blend into the golden grasses and become a part of the marsh itself. In the distance, I can see pearl-like specks that I know are egrets patiently stalking their dinner. Closer by, I watch an oystercatcher parading on a little spit of sand. The clown-like black and white bird with its distinctive orange beak is no doubt guarding a nest tucked in the matted grass. Close to my feet, hermit crabs poke their heads out of embanked holes in the sand, occasionally darting out to the water's edge for mysterious reasons of their own. Behind me, I hear seaside sparrows busily searching the grass for the small insects that make up their diet. And all around me is the quiet, never-ending rustle of the marsh grass sounding, as the breeze gently moves it, like the breath of a living being.

The marsh cordgrass, known by the scientific name *Spartina alterniflora* is, in fact, the breath of the salt marsh—its breath and its soul. There are other grasses growing behind the cordgrass—the tall and stately phragmites, whose feathery plumes reach toward the sky; black needlerush, or *Juncus roemerianus*, whose needle-like leaves were used by early settlers for sewing, and salt meadow hay, or *Spartina patens*, a popular food for the Ocracoke ponies and other herbivores.

But the marsh cordgrass is the material with which the tapestry of the salt marsh is woven. Its root system, composed of rhizomes, spreads out like a net as it grows. When it and other marsh plants die, they are caught in this net. As they gradually decay, they turn into rich, alluvial soil, building more salt marsh and constantly expanding into the sound.

Cordgrass is one of the few plants able to survive in the harsh environment at the edge of the marsh. It lives in the sub-tidal zone, which is inundated by estuary water at each high tide. Its roots, therefore, are submerged in an anaerobic (lacking oxygen) condition, and are unable to collect oxygen for respiration and metabolism as most plants do. In order to get oxygen to the submerged roots, *Spartina alternaflora* has a series of hollow tubes running down the stems to the roots. Trapdoor-like openings in the leaves, called stomata, close at high tide to prevent these tubes from filling with water.

Marsh cordgrass also has special adaptations to survive the high salinity levels in the water. Whereas most plants would lose the water in their cells through osmosis in such a saline environment, thus drying up and dying, cordgrass maintains a higher salt level in its cells than the salt level in the surrounding water. Special membranes in the roots and glands on the leaves prevent the salt level from becoming too high.

The cordgrass forms a dense and protective habitat for many marsh residents. Ribbed mussels cling to its roots, forming grape-like clusters. They introduce nitrogen and phosphate into the marsh ecosystem as they filter water. Chocolate-colored marsh crabs eat the grass as it emerges from the murky marsh bottom. Farther up the stalks, tiny snails, known as periwinkles, live. They travel up and down the stalks in perfect synchronism with the rising and falling tides, scraping off and ingesting algae as they go.

Secretive rails and bitterns stalk insects, snails, and small crustaceans along pathways in the dense grass. Residents of the upper marsh, such as meadow mice, sharp-tailed sparrows, and minks, visit the cordgrass zone to search for nesting materials and food. Marsh hawks, also known as harriers, swoop down to seize them, finding their own dinner in the marsh grass.

We know that salt marshes, along with other wetlands, are

an extremely important part of our ecosystem. The marshes filter and clean our ground water, provide flood control, and provide vital habitat, not only for the permanent marsh dwellers, but for many of our ocean and estuary species as well. Young fish and shrimp find food and shelter in this ambiguous zone where the land emerges from the sea. Cordgrass breaks down as it dies and becomes an important food source, known as detritus, for myriad species of aquatic life.

Development has gradually eaten up many of our coastal marshes, and pollution has degraded many others. Scientists and legislators, belatedly recognizing the ecological significance of the salt marshes, have taken measures to conserve them. Today, they are protected under the Clean Water and Coastal Area Management Acts. Loopholes in the laws, however, still allow marshlands to be filled, paved, and destroyed, and they are gradually disappearing. This stretch of natural, untouched salt marsh is one of Ocracoke's greatest treasures.

So I sit at the water's edge, lulled by the rustling of the marsh grass, savoring this golden afternoon. No, the marsh is not spectacular or dramatic, like the crashing surf of the ocean. But it is, in Sidney Lanier's words, "candid and simple, nothing-withholding, and free." I like to think that if I stop here for a while, I might take back some of these qualities myself.

A New Perspective on Clams

With my recently purchased commercial clam license in hand and an old pair of tennis shoes thrown over my shoulder, I pedaled my bicycle along the road that winds around Silver Lake Harbor. It was dawn, and the sun was just tinting the eastern sky with a soft rose patina. The amused chortle of laughing gulls resounded in my ears. Across the harbor, sailboat masts swayed in the breeze at the Community Store dock, and I saw a flicker of motion as someone prepared for departure. I slowed down as a great egret, frightened by my passing, soared overhead, its yellow beak and black legs in sharp contrast to its white plumage.

I didn't pause for long, however, as I was eager to reach my destination. Soon, I arrived at Wayne Teeter's Fish House, tucked next to the mouth of the harbor. Laying my bicycle in the marsh grass, I picked my way over to the little dock near where Arlene Burley's boat was anchored. In my anticipation, I had arrived early, so I sat down on the dock to wait.

This was the big day—the start of my new career as a "commercial clammer" on Ocracoke. I was out to make my fortune on those succulent little mollusks known in the North as quahogs and in the South as hard-shelled clams. As I sat there, watching a wooden skiff pass by with a load of crab pots, I thought about my plans. I knew a little about clamming, having raked quite a few dinners in the tidal flats north of Oyster Creek on warm summer days.

I knew that clams are bivalves, belonging to the phylum *Mollusca*. They have an exoskeleton composed of two calcareous, or limestone-like, shells. They live under the sand or mud in brackish or salt water from the Gulf of Maine to the Gulf of Mexico. I also knew that there were three sizes of clams. Littlenecks, up to one-and-a-half inches across, derive their name from the siphons that move water in and out of their systems. Cherrystones, two to two-and-a-half inches across, are named for the Eastern Shore creek in Virginia famous for its clams. The biggest ones, four inches or more, are called chowder clams, since they are best eaten in soups.

I knew that clamming is best at low tide, when it is easiest to rake or "tread" the clams with your toes, as they use their hatchet-shaped "feet" to move close to the surface. And I knew how delicious they tasted, roasted on a grill with lemon and butter, dipped in a cornmeal batter and fried with hush puppies, or simmered with broth in a savory Ocracoke chowder. But now I was ready to learn the serious business of earning a living from the little mollusks.

I didn't have long to wait. Soon, I heard the creak of a bicycle wheel, and Arlene rode up. I helped her load two clam rakes and

clam boxes into the boat, and we were off. I paid careful attention as she showed me how to start and steer the boat, maneuvering through the channel, over the flats, and out to Hog Shoal. It was May, early in the season, and the clams would be buried deeper in the mud than in summer; but she assured me that we would still bring back a good load.

I couldn't wait to begin. We anchored the boat, hopped into the waist-high water, and tied the boxes to our middles with ropes. "Let's go," shouted Arlene, pushing a clam rake in front of her. Before long she reached down and pulled up a healthy-looking clam.

I copied her enthusiastically, but all I dug up were broken shells. She showed me how to tell the difference between the solid "clunk" that the rake made when it hit a live clam, and the empty "click" made by an empty shell. I imitated her precisely, but for all her "clunks," I got only "clicks."

"Don't worry," she encouraged me. "It just takes time. You'll get the hang of it soon."

I watched wistfully as her box filled up.

Click.

I bent over and picked up another empty clam shell. I turned it over in my hand, momentarily forgetting my mission as I admired the purple sheen of its lining. The native people who originally lived in this area—the Croatan and Wococon Indians—would have prized this shell. They would have ground it into disc-shaped beads for belts and jewelry and used it as "roanoke" or "wampum"—their form of money. They used it for trading among themselves, with other tribes, and with Europeans when they came to this country. So widespread was the use of "wampum shell" money that the Dutch made it legal currency when they governed New Amsterdam—until America's first counterfeiting business was set up on Long Island. It was this latter use that gave the hard-shelled clam its scientific name—*Mercenaria mercenaria*.

But I'd never fill my box daydreaming like this. Too bad, I thought ruefully, that the empty shells couldn't be used as money today. I'd be on my way to a fortune.

I pushed on, forcing my rake as far as it would go, struggling until I was exhausted. Finally I felt a solid "clunk" and reaching down into the mud, I lifted out a live clam.

Hallelujah!

I held it up, examining the concentric ridges on its thick, whitish, oval shell. I tried to pry it open, though I knew that the adductor muscles, which held it clamped tight, were incredibly strong. It is this trait that led to its common name, "clam," as well as such phrases as "clam up" and "tight as a clam."

When the clam is in the mud, the muscles relax, allowing the two siphons to extend up and force water in and out. Known as a filter feeder, it extracts plankton and oxygen from the water, providing the important ecological service of cleansing the water in the process.

I tossed the clam into my box. My luck did not continue, however. No more wonderful "clunks" met my clam rake. I began to daydream again, this time wondering about the clam's reputation as an aphrodisiac. In tribute to its supposed powers, the artist Botticelli depicted Venus, the goddess of love, in a clam shell in his painting *The Birth of Venus*.

"Try over here, in this grass," suggested Arlene, still trying to encourage me. We had been clamming for two hours now, and Arlene had filled her first box and was working on another. My one clam looked very lonely.

Click.

I pulled up a broken whelk.

Click.

This time, another scallop.

Clunk.

That's it! I carefully lifted it out, a whopper, at least four inches across.

I wondered how old it was. Clams can live for as long as 25 years. I imagined it back in its infancy. It began its life as an egg, expelled by a female clam into the water, where it would be fertilized externally by a nearby male, along with 240 million or so siblings. It would have spent the first stage of its life as a free-swimming trocophore, evolving into a veliger larva. In this form it secreted its shell, settling down on the bottom to begin its life as an a clam. It would take approximately two to four years to reach adulthood.

I tossed it into my box, but as the morning progressed, my enthusiasm waned. I began to think that clamming for a living might not be such a great idea after all.

Even Arlene's encouraging remarks were losing their conviction. I found myself admiring the diving sandwich terns and dreaming about lunch. (Not, mind you, clam chowder.)

Pushing my rake half-heartedly, I felt one last "clunk." I picked up the clam and, gazing at it sadly, tossed it into Arlene's box. Then we sloshed back to the boat in silent agreement that I was not destined to be a commercial clammer.

The sun was high now, and it was a beautiful day. In spite of my disastrous failure in the clamming business, I felt good. Arlene and I talked and laughed as the boat skimmed over the glassy surface of Pamlico Sound. She had a good load of clams to sell, and I had a new perspective on clams.

I had developed a healthy respect for the tough little mollusks as I sloshed through their home territory. I hoped that pollution and over-harvesting, which had already decimated their sister bivalves, the oysters, would not destroy them. Remembering the important role they play in the ecosystem of the sound and the wonderfully tasty meals they provide, I wished them well. As we pulled up next to the dock in Silver Lake Harbor, Arlene and I were, you might say, "as happy as clams."

Harbingers of Spring: Baby Songbirds

Summer is almost here, and what a relief. No more waking up at six in the morning. No more hourly feeding vigils. No more private lessons on how to be a bird. Nesting season for Ocracoke's songbirds was finally over.

Among all the wondrous joys of springtime, probably my favorite is the chorus of birdsong that fills the air and the industrious activity that accompanies it. Male robins, house wrens, and warblers, newly arrived from their wintering grounds to the south, stake out territories with a variety of calls, whistles, and songs. Soon, as their potential mates arrive, they pair off and begin building nests. And what more thrilling sight exists than a newly leafed tree that wears, to quote Joyce Kilmer, "a nest of robins in its hair?"

But all those adorable baby birds (called nestlings) get hungry and restless, and that's when the trouble starts. In all the jostling and grabbing for the best worms that Mama Bird brings to the nest, someone is likely to fall out. An ominous fate awaits those over-zealous youngsters who are too young to fly or fend for themselves. Hungry cats, stealthy crows, cold nights, and eventual starvation allow them little chance of survival.

Enter the human being, strolling along, minding her own business. Who hasn't, sometime in life, discovered a pitiful, helpless baby bird cheeping on the ground, and wanted to help? If you were wise (or lucky) enough to ignore the old wives' tale that parent birds will desert a baby touched by human hands, you returned it to its nest. Or if it was old enough to have feathers, you locked up the neighborhood cats, made sure Mama and Papa Birds were around, and left it to their care. Then you went merrily along your way, having done your good deed for the day.

But if you couldn't find the nest, felt the bird was in immediate danger, or thought that it would be "fun" to raise a baby bird, well, you probably know what I'm talking about. As a wildlife rehabilitator, I am the recipient of most of Ocracoke's avian foundlings, and in the spring my home is converted into the "Friendly Feathered Family Orphanage."

From the moment I receive that phone call, "Pat, I found this baby bird," until it flies away a month or two later, my work is cut out for me.

First, I prepare a cage, preferably a box or old aquarium, with newsprint on the bottom and a nest made from a strawberry basket, lined with Kleenex. When the nestling arrives, I try to identify it, a difficult but important task, since different birds require different diets. I use a specially prepared baby bird formula, which I buy from a pet store, and add cooked egg yolk, peanut butter, high quality cat food, yogurt, or mealworms, depending on the species.

Most nestlings will holler to let you know when they're hungry, and gape (open their mouths wide enough to swallow a whale), so it's easy to feed them with a blunt stick or eye dropper. The problem is that they have to eat so often, at least every half hour for very young ones. This means that I have to take them with me everywhere I go, and excuse myself at even the most important engagements. ("You don't mind holding up this meeting, do you, while I feed my warbler?") Thank goodness, they sleep at night.

Feeding is not the only responsibility, of course. What goes in must come out, which means the nest and cage must be cleaned several times a day. As they grow older, nestlings must be provided with opportunities to learn to fly, to scrounge for sticks and pebbles, and to eat on their own. I tempt them with all kinds of delectable delicacies: mealworms, earthworms, strawberries, apples, and beetles, to name a few. We have contests of willpower as they jump up and down with their mouths open wide, insisting that I feed them, while I try to hold out, insisting that they do it themselves. They always seem to win, but somehow, eventually, they learn to eat on their own, as well as to fly and to fend for themselves.

Fortunately, there are rewards for all this. Baby birds make amazing alarm clocks. I never oversleep during nesting season (though, of course, they set the clocks, and their idea of "rise and shine" comes hours before mine). They keep me on my toes all day, reminding me when each new hour arrives. They give me a rather comforting feeling of being needed, and they are, I have to admit, awfully cute. The ultimate reward, of course, is to watch them fly away to freedom, adding their voices to that glorious symphony in the trees.

Many people, when they think of birds on the Outer Banks, visualize water birds such as gulls, herons, and pelicans. But there are, in fact, an amazing number and variety of passerines, or songbirds, here as well. Passerines, belonging to the order Passeriformes, are the perching birds. They have four toes, three facing forward, one backward. They are the most familiar and prolific of the avian orders. The National Park Service census lists over a hundred species of passerines regularly observed on the Outer Banks.

These are known as neotropical migratory birds. They may spend their winters in South or Central America and come to North Carolina to breed, as does the eastern phoebe. Or they may winter here and fly north to New England or Canada for breeding season, as does the savannah sparrow. Some, such as the cedar waxwing, which adorns the juniper trees here like decorations on Christmas trees, only pass through on their way to their final destination. Others, such as the cardinal and chickadee, participate in what is known as leapfrog migration, overlapping their ranges. The cardinal that eats at your bird feeder in the winter may fly north to nest, while another cardinal, which spent its winter in Florida, may raise its family in your yard. Some of the birds may not migrate at all but stay in one area all year if the conditions are auspicious. Scientists still have lots of unanswered questions about their life histories.

One thing they do know is that many of our songbirds are declining at an alarming rate. Pesticides, which saturate the insects and seeds that comprise much of their diet, sometimes destroy whole flocks of birds. Not as noticeable, but just as serious, is the slow insidious poisoning of birds. This doesn't kill them outright but affects their immune systems and reproductive abilities. The Environmental Protection Agency attempts to regulate pesticides that cause high bird mortality, but sometimes a lot of songbirds die before a pesticide is prohibited. An example of this is the insecticide granular carbofuran, which was restricted in this country in 1991, but not until it had killed approximately a million birds a year while in use.

Automobiles destroy a number of songbirds, as do BB guns in irresponsible hands. It is a federal offense to kill any songbird or other migratory bird in this country. Each year large numbers of passerines die as a result of flying into glass windows and doors that they fail to see. Installing shaded glass and hanging plants or other objects to make the glass more obvious can reduce these mortalities.

One important culprit is the domestic cat. One house cat, allowed to roam outdoors, will kill several hundred birds and small mammals in a year, according to the Humane Society. Feral cats kill even more. These cats are not a natural part of the environment in America. And while it is not a cat's fault for obeying its instincts and hunting birds, it is our responsibility as cat owners to prevent cats from further decimating our bird population.

Brown-headed cowbirds, which have worked their way east from the midwest as forests have been cut down, are also a problem. These birds, which are becoming a common sight at many bird feeders, lay their eggs in the nests of songbirds, some of which are becoming endangered. The larger, more aggressive cowbird babies force out the original nestlings, and the mother songbirds raise the cowbird babies instead.

The main cause of songbird decline is loss of habitat, not only in North America, but in South and Central America where the birds winter. The growth of cities and suburbs leads to the clearing of forests and destruction of other bird habitats, and infringes on songbird territories. While some birds, such as cardinals and mockingbirds, seem to thrive in back yards, others, such as Bachman's warblers, which are close to extinction, require virgin forests and solitude. Even such intrusions as jet planes flying overhead may affect their survival.

To the south, the destruction of the rain forests has a tremendous impact on our songbirds. Even if conditions are optimal for birds here, they will die if they find their winter homes cut down and burned.

That is why an important new concept in conservation has developed. Known as "Partners in Flight," it is a unique cooperative movement among all the states and nations where songbirds live or pass through. Its goal is to study and protect the birds along their entire flyway. It includes government agencies, environmental and birding organizations, scientists, and businessmen. It is an excellent example of how people everywhere can work together to protect the interconnected pieces of the earth.

Each one of us can play a part in this movement by learning about the birds in our neighborhood, and how to protect and provide for them. We can put up bird houses and feeders, and make sure the birds have fresh water. We can restrain our cats, birdproof our windows, and remind our children to use their BB guns on tin cans. We can join organizations that work to protect our wildlife and our environment, and last but not least, we can rescue injured and orphaned birds and deliver them to the proper caretakers. By doing these things, we can ensure that Rachel Carson's nightmare of a "silent spring," in which no birds sing, never comes to pass.

I guess that's why I think it's worth it to wake up at dawn and spend my days playing surrogate Mom to noisy, demanding baby birds. But wait, I have to stop. I hear my last mockingbird calling me: "It's lunchtime again, and I'm hungry. Make it snappy!"

"All right, all right. I'm coming!"

Tracks in the Sand:
Loggerhead Turtle Nesting

They looked like bulldozer tracks, plowing through the damp, cream-colored sand. Originating in the foamy surf, they meandered to the edge of a grass-covered dune, then returned to the sea. An unsuspecting observer might guess that they were made by some amphibious tank, churning out of the water. One might even imagine them to be tracks left behind by a sea monster creeping onto shore.

But I knew what the tracks meant, and I was thrilled to see them this early June morning. I, with others like me, had risen at daybreak for several weeks to drive along the shoreline, searching for them. They were the marks, known to scientists as a "crawl," of a female loggerhead sea turtle coming ashore to lay her eggs.

If you looked carefully, you could see the spot where she had dug out the sand at the edge of the dune and carefully replaced it. I knew that about 20 inches below the surface there would be a hollowed-out nest containing 80 to 150 golf-ball–shaped, leathery eggs, each holding the promise of life for a loggerhead turtle.

I was working as part of a team trying to locate and protect the nests of these turtles. Earlier in the spring, we had attended a workshop hosted by the National Park Service and the North Carolina Wildlife Commission. We learned how to distinguish the different kinds of turtles, how to locate and label the nests, and what to do if the nests were subject to heavy traffic or flooding and needed to be moved.

Loggerheads are one of five species of sea turtles that live along the Atlantic Coast and are protected under the Endangered Species Act of 1973. Most countries have banned the killing of sea turtles and the trade in their products.

The leatherback is the largest of these turtles. It can grow to more than eight feet in length and weigh as much as 1,300 pounds. It lacks the hard carapace, or upper shell, that most turtles have.

The smallest and most endangered of the sea turtles is the Kemps Ridley, which seldom reaches 100 pounds or exceeds two feet in length.

The Hawksbill, also a small turtle, has a beak-shaped head and a heart-shaped carapace. Hawksbills are sometimes killed for their shells, which are used to make "tortoise-shell" combs and other items.

The green turtle gets its name from the color of its fat, once popular in turtle soup. It is a gentle vegetarian, up to three feet long and weighing about 300 pounds.

Loggerheads are the most common sea turtles along the North Carolina coast. They have reddish carapaces and large log-like heads. Adults are about three feet long and weigh from 250 to 300 pounds. They are omnivorous, eating everything from hermit crabs to shellfish and the deadly Portuguese man-o'-war. Great wanderers, loggerheads journey many miles throughout the year. Each spring, however, finds some of them at their nesting grounds on the beach at Ocracoke Island.

I was confident that this crawl had been made by a loggerhead, because they are the only sea turtles that regularly nest in North Carolina. This one had no doubt mated in the surf earlier in the spring, then lingered in the waters offshore until the time and temperature were right. She struggled ashore during the night, using her flippers to pull herself along. When she found the right spot, based perhaps on the temperature of the sand, she used her hind flippers to dig the egg chamber. It probably took about an hour and a half for her to lay her eggs. She then carefully covered them with sand and waddled back to the ocean.

Loggerheads breed every two to three years. They come ashore several times during the nesting season to lay their eggs. It is believed that they return to their place of birth to nest, often traveling thousands of miles to get there. North Carolina is the northern edge of their nesting territory.

Beach development has drastically reduced the nesting sites for sea turtles, but that is only one reason that they are facing extinction. Ingestion of plastics and other man-made objects kills some turtles. Others drown in the nets used by commercial fishermen. While they can stay submerged for 30 to 40 minutes, sea turtles can't breathe under water and must come up for air.

Our efforts to protect the nests at Ocracoke are only one part of a worldwide movement to save these turtles. Concerned scientists and volunteers monitor nests in many countries to ensure the successful hatching of new generations. A "Turtle Stranding Network" helps to locate and document dead turtles so that the causes of death can be identified and, it is hoped, prevented. Public education programs inform people that litter and pollution bring death to sea turtles and other animals.

Scientists, government officials, and the fishing industry are trying to develop a workable plan to prevent sea turtles from drowning in shrimping and fishing nets. "Turtle Excluder Devices," known as TEDs, allow them to escape.

As I stood looking at the crawl on this June morning, the wind was sweeping along the shore and the tide was coming in. Soon they would wash away all signs of the turtle's arduous trek up the beach. By evening no one would be able to read the story written in the sand before me.

Just as the actions of nature would erase the tracks of the turtle, would the actions of humans, I wondered, eradicate the turtles themselves? Would the next decades find the ocean as barren of life as this strip of beach would be tonight? Would all our efforts to protect the sea turtles be in vain?

I looked at the beautiful morning—at the sea, the sand, the nest at my feet. Hidden and protected, the eggs within the nest were the seeds of hope, not only for the loggerhead turtle, but also for all life, for Earth itself. I pushed a stake into the ground to mark the nest and turned back to my truck, full of hope and looking forward to the awakening day.

A Living Flash of Light:
The Dragonfly

I was sitting quietly in my kayak, resting my arms after a strenuous paddle through one of Ocracoke's winding creeks. As I gazed out across the marsh toward Pamlico Sound, I lapped one hand lazily through the water.

Suddenly, I caught my breath. There, poised on the palm of my other hand, was an exquisite creature.

I moved slowly so that I could see it closer. It didn't seem afraid; indeed, it seemed quite at home as it clung to a finger with a feather-like touch. Its gossamer wings and iridescent hues gave it an other-worldly quality, like a magical visitor from a childhood world of fairies and dragons.

It was a dragonfly, known to entomologists by the scientific name of *Odonata* and described by nineteenth century poet Alfred Tennyson as "a living flash of light." To the Hopi Indians of Arizona, it is a religious symbol for life. To indigenous tribes in South America, it is a departed human spirit. Medieval English folk claimed that its needle-like form could be used to sew up the mouths of naughty children. Some Asian cultures claim that it makes a delectable dish when stir-fried in a wok. To Thomas Moffet, admiring the dragonfly more than 300 years ago, it "set forth Nature's elegancy beyond the expression of Art."

But dragonflies inhabited the earth long before the time of art or humans. Before the dinosaurs, 300 million years ago, giant dragonflies with wingspans approaching three feet hovered over swamps and bogs, the largest flying insects of all time.

Although they are the oldest surviving order of flying insects, dragonflies spend only a few weeks in the sky, wind, and light. For most of their lives—two to five years—they scrounge along the bottoms of creeks and marshes in the form of squat, mud-colored larvae, known as nymphs. Described by naturalist Edwin Way Teale as "blood-thirsty ogres," these nymphs consume any living creatures they can find, seizing them with a bottom lip that extends half the length of their bodies. Normally slow-moving, at times they shoot rapidly along the bottom, using a jet-propulsion system that expels water from a rear orifice.

They moult several times as they continue to eat and grow. Finally, one warm summer day, they climb out of the water along a plant stalk. There, in Cinderella fashion, they emerge from their ugly rags into ethereal creatures wearing, in Tennyson's words, "clear plates of sapphire mail."

Once they have attained their wings, dragonflies make amazing aviators. They have a built-in flight stabilizing mechanism, which enables them to fly in all directions, like a helicopter. In fact, Havasupai Indian children, who watch the antics of these insects at the bottom of the Grand Canyon, use the identical word for helicopters as for dragonflies.

Dragonflies reach speeds of 30 miles per hour as they pursue their prey, and they are able to detect small insects at distances of 40 feet with their huge, multi-faceted eyes. They go through dramatic courtship rituals, mating in mid-air, after which the female deposits her eggs in the water. They can be quite territorial and aggressive toward other dragonflies, but are harmless to humans. They are generally larger and more colorful than their cousins, the damsel flies.

On Ocracoke Island, dragonflies are especially welcome because of their culinary taste. Their favorite food seems to be those irritating, omnipresent, blood-sucking mosquitoes. In their larval stage, they consume large numbers of mosquito "wrigglers," more than 20 per minute. Adult dragonflies, often called mosquito hawks, have been found with their jaws so full of these pests that they couldn't close their mouths.

As I sat in my kayak observing my dragonfly visitor, however, it was not his voracious appetite that intrigued me. I felt honored that this regal creature had chosen my hand as its throne. It brought me a gift, inviting me, at least for a few moments, into its unique world of air, light, and magical flight. I whispered "thank you" as it gently released my hand and rose into the blue dome of the sky.

Summer

Memories of Childhood:
Blue Crabs

One of the earliest memories I have of the Outer Banks is of two pet blue crabs belonging (at least temporarily) to my cousin Ellen and me. We were probably not more than four years old, and the fact that they had pincers almost as big as our hands and were quite ready to use them on everyone did nothing to deter our affection for them.

My Uncle Bill had caught them, using that time-honored method of dangling a chicken neck from a string and scooping up the crabs with a fish net. He brought them back to the cottage we were renting at Nags Head, fully intending to steam them in vinegar and boiling water, along with a bushel or so of their brethren.

Ellen and I pleaded for their lives and were rewarded with temporary custody. We built them an elegant castle of sand, and lavished them with loving care. It seems that we had them for a long time, but I have a feeling that it was just until the next high tide washed the castle, along with its occupants, back out to sea.

At any rate, I have always had a fondness for *Callinectes sapidus*, the common blue crab found in great numbers here at Ocracoke and elsewhere on the mid-Atlantic coast.

I cherish memories of crabbing with my family at estuary creeks in Virginia and North Carolina as a teenager. I love to watch them scurry sideways beneath my little sailboat in Pamlico Sound or scull along in the waves at the ocean shore. I'm amazed by the ferocity displayed in fencing matches between angry male "jimmies." I'm impressed by the tender care they bestow on defenseless moulting females, or "sooks," so touchingly described in William Warner's award-winning book *Beautiful Swimmers*. And, needless to say, I could never insult them by turning down the offer of a half-bushel or so for steaming or picking!

Blue crabs are crustaceans, belonging to the same class as their equally delectable cousins, shrimp and lobsters. They have a hard exoskeleton, or carapace, made of chitin and calcium, which they discard, or moult, as they grow. Two bulbous eyes are attached to stems at the front of the carapace. They have two intimidating claws—blue in adult males—from which they derive their nickname "blue" or "blue-clawed" crab. The last of their four pairs of walking legs is modified into a pair of swimming paddles.

Unlike most crabs, they are excellent swimmers, which accounts for the first part of their scientific name. *Callinectes* means "beautiful swimmer" in Greek. The second part is not so romantic, but it is certainly accurate. *Sapidus* is Latin for tasty or delicious!

Adult males are larger than females and are easily distinguished by the shape of the "aprons" on their abdomens. The males' aprons are narrow, with two pairs of pleopods used in copulation. Those of the females are much wider and have numerous pleopods which are used to carry the eggs.

Blue crabs are scavengers, devouring dead fish, plant matter, and almost anything they can find (including, of course, chicken necks). They also prey on small fish and invertebrates.

They begin their lives in the late spring or summer, hatching from egg masses called "sponges" carried under the sooks' aprons, often a million or more at a time. They emerge as small, semi-transparent zoea larvae which become part of the plankton, drifting, eating voraciously, and moulting until they develop into megalops, which resemble small, bug-eyed lobsters. They continue to drift with the currents, moving toward the west side of the sound, developing into small crabs which reach sexual maturity between 12 and 16 months. They bury themselves in the substrate of the sound during the winter, and mate the following spring and summer. At this time, the male finds a nearly mature female and proceeds to court her. Raising up on tiptoe, he waves his swimming legs and snaps his body until the female indicates that she is duly impressed. He then wraps her in a cradle position and carries her around quite tenderly for several days until she is ready to moult. During this process, known as the "soft-shell" stage, he stands guard over her, forming a protective cage with his walking legs.

Mating takes place immediately after the female sheds, lasting for up to 12 hours. The male continues to protect the female until her new shell is fully hardened, which may take several more days. The female then begins moving east toward the inlets and ocean, which contain the saline water needed for her eggs to develop. During the summer and fall, her egg sponge changes from orange to brownish black. When it is time for her to spawn, the eggs are gradually abraded off by her movements, and she is ready to hibernate again when winter comes.

Springtime in the Pamlico Sound is announced not only by the arrival of innumerable blue crabs, but also by the appearance of hundreds of crab pots, marked with colorful floats, buoys, plastic bottles, or practically anything that will float. Crabbing is an important livelihood on the Outer Banks, particularly in spring and fall. Most of the crabs caught here are sooks on their way to or from the salty waters of the ocean.

Most crabbers at Ocracoke set their pots in late February and leave them out until June. There is a short summer season starting in late July, and the fall season begins in September or October. When water temperatures drop below 50 degrees, the crabs bury themselves in the soft mud of the sound to spend the winter.

Crab pots are square, wire cages which have several openings into which crabs can enter but from which they cannot escape. They are baited with scrap fish, often menhaden or croaker. For some mysterious reason, crabs seem to prefer different colors at different times and in different conditions, so a crabber's collection of crab pots is liable to include reds, yellows, blues, and blacks—a veritable rainbow of colors.

The crabbers use skiffs 18 to 20 feet long to set and check their lines of pots. They sell their catch to Murray Fulcher or Wayne Teeter, owners of the two local seafood houses. Frog Island Seafood sends trucks over from Elizabeth City to purchase the crabs, and in turn, they sell them on the mainland to processing plants where the meat is picked out and distributed to restaurants, grocery stores, and seafood markets.

There is probably no other animal that so truly symbolizes the bays and sounds of the mid-Atlantic as *Callinectes sapidus*. Aggressive, pugnacious, and hostile as it may be, it is, in its way, one of the most beloved of coastal creatures. It brings back memories of slower, simpler days, of childhood summers spent lazing in the sun, wading barefoot in brackish creeks, and catching dinner with a fish net, a string, and a chicken neck.

Medical Miracle of the Pamlico: Horseshoe Crabs

One day in early summer, I got a hankering for fried clams. I checked the tide chart, pulled the clam rake out from under the house, and hoisted it over my shoulder.

There was a section of tidal flat out behind Ocracoke Island, not far from where I lived, where I especially liked to go. The salt marsh curved around it, a blanket of soft gold adorned with white ibis and little blue herons. On the shallow bottom, you could watch scurrying hermit crabs and see an occasional hog-nosed skate. I walked out through the dark, knee-deep water, heading for my favorite clamming spot.

Suddenly, I realized that I was not alone. I was completely surrounded by alien-like creatures, three to four feet long. I resisted the urge to panic and took a closer look, which revealed that they were not one creature, but two.

Small, brown, helmet-shaped animals rode piggyback behind similar larger ones. Paying little attention to me, they scuttled across the sandy bottom, intent on business of their own. But I knew what they were about. The tidal flat was a giant ballroom, full of courting horseshoe crabs!

They looked forbidding with their large jagged shells and spike-like tails, or telsons, but I knew that they were quite harmless. The females, up to two feet in length, were heading for shore where, at high tide, they would deposit hundreds of eggs in shallow depressions in the sand. The smaller males were hitching free rides to the spawning area. There, they would release sperm into the water, fertilizing the eggs. This act would be repeated again and again until thousands of small round greenish eggs were laid, ready to hatch in a couple of weeks on another high tide.

Horseshoe crabs, or *Limulus polyphemus*, are not actually crabs at all. They are more closely related to spiders and ticks, belonging to the class Arachnida and the sub-phylum Chelicerata. Often called "living fossils," they have changed little since the time of their ancestors, the Eurypterids, which lived in Devonian seas 350 million years ago.

They have helmet-shaped shells, or carapaces, segmented into three parts: the cephalothorax, the abdomen, and the telson, or tail spine. Four eyes, two compound and two simple, are located on the top, or dorsal, side. On the underside are a number of appendages which play various roles.

The chelicerae, located at the front, are used to capture prey, usually worms or mollusks buried in the substrate. They deposit the food in the ganthbase, which is found at the point where the crab's five walking legs are attached. The movement of the legs as the crab walks masticates the food so that the crab can ingest it. Horseshoe crabs always eat "on the run."

The first pair of legs, known as pedipalpi, are used not only for walking but also by the males for clinging to the females. The fifth pair is used for digging, pushing the crab along, and cleaning the gills. The gills, which fold like pages of a book, are used for breathing and swimming, often upside down.

Horseshoe crabs use their long spine-like telsons to flip themselves over if they somehow get stranded on their backs. As dangerous as it looks, the telson is apparently not used as a weapon.

These strange creatures may live for 15 to 20 years. They hatch out as tiny, tailless "trilobite larvae," so named because of their resemblance to their ancient relatives. They crawl to the water where, swimming on their backs, they feed on microscopic organisms at the bottom. As they grow, they shed their old shells, eyes included. They moult several times a year at first, later once a year. It is these moulted carapaces that beachcombers often find along the shores of ocean and sound.

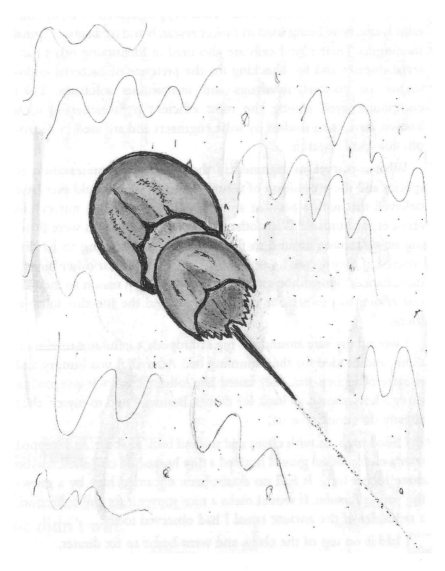

Human beings have found many uses for horseshoe crabs over the years. Native Americans used the telsons as spears and ate the flesh. Anglo-Americans ground them up for fertilizer and chicken feed, and they still use them for lobster bait.

The unique physiology of horseshoe crabs is proving to be extremely important in modern medicine and science. Their "blue blood" (which receives its color from copper instead of iron) contains lysate, now being used in cancer research and to diagnose spinal meningitis. Their blood cells are also used in identifying other bacterial diseases and for checking for the presence of bacterial endotoxins, or poisons, in drugs and intravenous solutions. Their compound eyes, among the most efficient light-gathering tools known, have been studied by solar engineers and are used in neurophysiological research.

What a marvelous argument, I thought, for the preservation of species and the promotion of natural diversity. Who would ever have believed that such a peculiar animal could provide such miraculous services for humans? What other medical breakthroughs were floating or swimming around in these vast seas, just waiting to be discovered, if they weren't destroyed first by pollution or other human disturbances? Horseshoe crabs were another good reason to increase our efforts to protect our marine waters and the life that inhabits them.

I wound my way around the big arthropods, careful not to step on them, and headed for the clamming bed. After all, I was hungry, and in spite of reports that they tasted like lobster, I was not tempted to carry a horseshoe crab back for dinner. Besides, I said to myself, they already do enough for us.

I filled my sack with clams and sloshed back to shore. As I stepped over a clump of eel grass, I noticed a tiny horseshoe crab shell, maybe three inches long. It had no doubt been discarded here by a growing young *Limulus*. It would make a nice souvenir for my collection, a reminder of the ancient ritual I had observed today.

I laid it on top of the clams and went home to fix dinner.

Brown Pelicans:
A Success Story

"We're going to band pelicans Thursday," Mickey Baker said after pulling up behind my truck in the driveway. "Do you want to come?"

I had just returned to Ocracoke from a week with my parents in Virginia, and I had a ton of work to do. I had vowed that I would not do anything else until the work was finished.

"Sure, I'd love to," I told her.

We met at the public boat dock at seven that morning. There were 10 of us. John Weske, formerly with the U.S. Fish and Wildlife Service, now a research assistant at the Smithsonian, was in charge of the outing. He had been working on a banding project with royal terns since the 1970s, and with the pelicans since the mid-'80s. Assisting him today were Mike Browne from North Carolina State University and John Brunjes from the Audubon Society. The rest of us were volunteers from Ocracoke.

John ferried one boatload of people out to Beacon Island, then returned for the rest of us. We had been warned to wear heavy clothing, and sitting in the sun was making us hot already. The spray felt good as we bounced along across the waves in the little motorboat.

At our destination, we climbed over the side and sloshed through the hip-deep water onto the narrow ridge of sand where our companions waited. Hundreds of gulls hovered in the air, stirred off their nests by the human invasion. Behind them soared the larger forms of adult brown pelicans, gradually settling down on the water to await our departure. The cries of the laughing gulls sounded like a jeering crowd in a football stadium as we walked up the beach.

The little island was covered with salt grass, interspersed with the bright yellow flowers of sea ox-eye. Mud lay thick in some of the marshy areas, and there were open spots piled high with dried bird droppings, known as guano. We had no time for exploring. We had to work quickly, before the searing July sun became unbearable.

John explained the procedures.

The pelican chicks were congregated in small colonies. We would start by surrounding the closest group. Six of us would catch and hold the birds, keeping one hand wrapped around the huge beaks and using the other to restrain the wings. Four people would do the banding, using special pliers to firmly attach the rings of metal around each bird's right leg. As soon as one bird was done, we would release it and move on to the next. Speed was essential. We wanted to keep stress to a minimum and allow the parents to return to their young as soon as possible.

The nests were built on the ground and lined with grass. While most of the chicks had hatched, a few of the nests still contained two or three chalky white eggs. Some of the chicks, those still covered with white down, were too young to be banded. They squawked at us as we walked by. They were so incredibly ugly that they were cute. John called them "a perfect example of pelican beauty".

The older chicks tried to escape but soon became entangled in the grass or in a huddle of other pelicans. They were easy to catch and the work went quickly. We moved from colony to colony, banding some four hundred young pelicans in a few hours.

"Uh-oh!" I exclaimed, as one of the unhappy birds regurgitated his breakfast of fish onto my shirt.

"Now I know why the experts wear hats!" moaned another volunteer as she glared up at the laughing gull who had just passed over her head.

"Do I smell as bad as I think I do, or is it just my imagination?" I wondered out loud.

My companion, wondering the same thing, could not answer.

By the time we finished, we were not only hot, dirty, and smelly, but we were also exhausted. We gulped down the water in our canteens, and some of us immersed ourselves, fully dressed, in the cool waters of the sound.

As the boat pulled away, headed back to Ocracoke, we watched the relieved adult pelicans and gulls swoop back onto the sand spit, searching for their families. Soon, everything would be back to normal.

"I wonder if our visit will become part of pelican mythology," mused Barb Wagner, one of the volunteers.

Pelicans are one of the success stories of the environmental movement. The use of the pesticide DDT in the 1950s and '60s brought pelicans, along with a number of other birds, to the brink of extinction. DDT, ingested with the fish they ate, became concentrated in their systems, causing a calcium deficiency. Their eggshells were so thin that they broke before they could hatch, so no new pelicans were being born. By the late '60s, there were only ten pairs of brown pelicans left in North Carolina.

After DDT was banned, the pelicans began to make a comeback, expanding their numbers and their range. They moved into Virginia, north of their original territory, and are continuing to work their way northward.

"This is a new population," John explained. "It will be interesting to see what they do."

Almost everyone who visits the Outer Banks today is familiar with these huge, clown-like birds. They seem to like people and often follow boats or frequent piers, seeking handouts of fish scraps. They are often seen soaring low over the ocean in single-file formation, riding the drafts and searching for fish.

Brown pelicans, which received their name from the Greek word for woodpecker (referring to their remarkable beaks), grow to four feet in length, with a wingspread of up to six feet. They look like ancient pterodactyls as they soar above the ocean; they are, in fact, one of the most ancient of birds. They plunge-dive deep into the water to catch fish, using special air sacks under their skin to help them float back to the surface. Huge pouches under their beaks act as fish nets, helping them catch the fish, which they swallow whole or carry back to their young.

The chicks that we banded were born in late spring. It would take at least three years for them to reach breeding age. If unharmed, they would live 20 to 30 years.

John and Mike explained later, as we relaxed in my living room after cleaning up, that the information gathered in the banding program would provide more knowledge about migratory patterns, demographics, and life histories of the birds. This, in turn, would help determine management practices.

"If we understand how a healthy population of pelicans works, then if they get into trouble again, we'll better understand how to respond."

Whenever I see a pelican now, I wonder if it is wearing one of our little silver-colored bracelets. And I hope that I'll be seeing them for a long, long time.

Phantoms in the Surf: Ghost Crabs

Dark clouds gathered in the evening sky, pushed about by a warm, restless August wind. It was a perfect time for an evening stroll by the ocean. My friend Randy Powers was visiting, and even though rain was threatening, it only took a moment to agree to head for the beach.

We left the truck at the parking lot across from the Pony Pens and hiked across the dunes. Sea oats, tossed by the wind, brushed against our legs. The night was dark, stars and moon hidden by the clouds. As we reached the water's edge, great drops of rain began to fall. We tried to ignore them, but soon we were caught in a downpour. We bolted for the car.

As we sat out of the rain, shivering, dripping, and trying to decide what to do, the clouds broke apart, the rain stopped, and the full moon appeared, as if by magic, bathing us in light. Delighted, we headed back to the beach, now able to see clearly.

What we saw astounded us. The beach, which had been empty of life before, was alive with movement. There was barely room to walk. For as far as we could see, ghost crabs were advancing across the beach toward the ocean.

The pale land crabs streamed across the sands and into the surf, fighting against the waves as they crowded into the water. It was an incredible sight, and we watched for a long time before returning to the truck and driving back to the village. The next morning, the strange sight of the night before seemed like a dream.

My curiosity piqued, I began reading all the material I could find about ghost crabs. They are crustaceans, belonging to the phylum *Arthropoda*, along with insects, shrimp, and other creatures with chitin exoskeletons and jointed appendages. Their scientific name, *Ocypode quadrata*, means "swift feet." They can move up to six feet per second as they scuttle sideways across the sand.

Ghost crabs, which get their common name from the whitish translucence of their carapaces, are amphibious crabs on an "evolutionary trek" out of the water and onto land. Although they begin their lives in the water, they gradually move farther and farther ashore, returning to the ocean's edge only to feed and lay their eggs.

Adults have reduced gills that are capable of extracting oxygen from the air if kept wet. The crabs use hair-like setae on their legs to "vacuum" moisture out of the sand. The technique is the equivalent of a person drinking juice using a three-foot straw.

Ghost crabs live on sandy beaches from Delaware to Florida. They are one of a number of related species of land crabs that live in various areas of the world.

They are basically nocturnal, but beachgoers often see them in the morning or late afternoon when they build or repair their tunnel-like homes, carrying the sand between their small claw and first and second legs. During the hottest part of the day, they retire into their tunnels, which may descend four to six feet underground. Built at a 45-degree angle, the tunnels are often shaped like a U, a J, or a Y. Some have an extra tunnel which is used as an escape route or a mating chamber.

One hot lazy day as I lay reading on the beach, I felt a movement under my foot. Resisting the urge to jump, I looked down and watched as a ghost crab dug himself a comfortable retreat under my foot. For the next half hour, it foraged the beach, beating a hasty retreat under my toes whenever it was frightened or wanted to escape the hot sun.

After beginning their lives as eggs (somewhere between 20,000 and 200,000 are deposited by each female just beyond the surf), they hatch into zoea, which then develop into megalops, planktonic lar-

val stages that drift along the ocean shore for four to six weeks. They then develop into match-head size crabs and make their way ashore. Gradually, they work their way landward as they grow older, and fully mature crabs may live up to a quarter mile from the ocean.

Ghost crabs do most of their foraging at night. They feed mainly on coquina mollusks and mole crabs, which burrow along the wet sand at the tide line. They will eat almost anything they can find, however, including dead fish or birds, debris left by humans, or smaller crabs. They sometimes snatch hatchling sea turtles as they make their way to the ocean. In turn, ghost crabs are eaten by gulls, raccoons, and other predators. They are an important part of the seashore ecosystem, helping to keep the beaches clean.

Many a summer night, driving the road from the ferry landing to the village, I have dodged ghost crabs in the road, while wondering if the driver behind me thought I'd had a few too many. My readings explained to me why these crabs were there, looking lost and out of place. They find their way to the sea each night by following the light (it is always lighter over the ocean than over land). The lights of cars on the highway attract them, convincing them that the ocean is in the direction of the speeding cars. As a car approaches, the crab often freezes. Sometimes, it will even run toward the headlights. A busy night with lots of traffic will leave the road littered with ghost crab carcasses the next morning.

The crabs killed on the road probably do not have any real impact on the population. Beach development and the use of off-road vehicles at night, however, have devastating effects on land crabs. The red land crab, the southern cousin of the ghost crab, was completely wiped out in this country by development in the '70s.

Normal daytime beach use does not seem to have a detrimental effect on the crabs; indeed, they seem to thrive on the food litter left behind by fishermen and sunbathers. Nor is much harm caused by driving on the beach during the day when the crabs are safe in their tunnels. Studies show that even the heaviest vehicles do not crush the crabs when they are under the sand.

But driving on the beach at night, when the crabs are foraging, is devastating. A recent study done at Cape Lookout, south of Ocracoke Island, found that one vehicle killed 500 crabs in one evening's run from the lighthouse to the point. In areas of heavy night traffic, ghost crabs gradually disappear.

Finally, in all my reading, I found what I believe is the answer to the mystery of that strange ghost crab migration to the sea that Randy and I had happened upon.

Thomas G. and Donna L. Wolcott described the egg-laying behavior of female ghost crabs in their article "Wet Behind the Gills," which was printed in *The Caribbean*. Females descend to the ocean's edge and clamber into the waves to deposit their eggs in movements that are "often synchronous," they wrote, "and where populations are dense, spectacular."

Spectacular was a good word to describe the event we witnessed that night.

Shrimp: The Insects of the Sea

I was on my way to the beach on a hot summer afternoon, pedaling my bicycle along Silver Lake, when I saw what looked like a pair of giant antennae growing out of the roof of South Point Fish House. I knew what that meant. The "antennae" were actually outriggers. A shrimp boat was in.

Hitting the brake, I skidded to a halt, turned my bicycle around in the road and pulled up in front of one of the wide double doors. Sure enough, a gathering of people stood inside. I spotted Murray Fulcher, the owner, and asked if he could use another hand. After a quick count of heads, he nodded.

"Come on if you want to."

I forgot about the beach, forgot about my other plans for the afternoon. It was time to "head" shrimp.

This was in July, 1985, one of the best seasons for shrimp in years. I had started heading shrimp a few weeks before, when the first boats began pulling up at the dock to unload their catches. It was not your typical nine-to-five job; there were no regular hours or much notice either. When the weather was right, the shrimp boats went out. When the conditions were right, they caught shrimp. And when the holds were full, they came in. That was when my job started, and it lasted until the last shrimp was beheaded and packed in ice.

There were usually six or eight of us, and we stood around a long table on the dock. We all knew each other, Ocracoke being such a small place, and it was fun to get together and swap stories. While we talked, the shrimp kept coming, and we clipped the heads off, using our thumbs, and tossed them into buckets. The shrimp moved down the assembly line to the end where they were collected and set aside to be sold. We got paid by the bucket, so it behooved us to work as fast as we could.

It was fun trying to perfect your skill, using both hands. But the shrimp and water were ice-cold, and the acid from the shrimp stung your hands. Gloves slowed you down too much, so that didn't work very well. Most of us just "grinned and bore it."

Once the hold on the shrimp boat was empty, our job was finished, and I was ready to go home, soak my cold, smelly hands in warm water and lemon juice, and rub them with aloe. Afterwards, I would look forward to eating a delicious meal of very fresh chunks of sautéed shrimp. Murray always allowed us to throw the broken shrimp in a separate bucket to take home, a real bonus. I usually had enough for two or three dinners if I used them sparingly.

South Point doesn't process shrimp like that anymore, but it does still buy shrimp when the boats come in. This summer, only one local boat, the *Miss Miriam*, went shrimping, collecting enough for island markets, but not enough to be shipped out.

Shrimp are one of the most sought-after creatures in the seas, not only by humans but by myriad other hungry predators. Fortunately, they are also among the most abundant creatures, sometimes called the "insects of the seas" for this reason. Like their delicious cousins, the crabs and lobsters, they are classified as decopods, a name that refers to their ten legs. All of the decopods are crustaceans, members of the phylum *Arthropoda*.

Shrimp differ from most decopods in that they are good swimmers, using abdominal appendages known as pleopods to move forward and their tail fans to shoot rapidly backwards. Most are bottom-dwellers, living among the algae and sea grass, hiding under stones, and burrowing in the substrate. They eat small animals and plants, crushing them with huge mandibles. The females spawn in the spring and summer, producing up to a million eggs which are fertilized by sperm released into the water by the males. Free-swimming "nauplius" hatch out and join the giant mass of floating plankton. They go through several metamorphoses before emerging as full-grown shrimp.

Some, such as the white shrimp, are diurnal, searching for food during the day and burrowing at night. Others, such as the pink shrimp, are nocturnal, reversing the cycle. Most kinds of shrimp live in salt water, but there are a few species of freshwater shrimp, including one that reaches a weight of three pounds and lives in—you guessed it—Texas.

Some of the more highly specialized shrimp have developed fascinating adaptations to help them survive. Some, such as *Hippolyte varians*, can change color at will. By expanding and contracting their chromatophores, they can adapt their pigmentation to blend in with the seaweed or light conditions. Sergestes shrimp have light-emitting organs, known as photophores, which produce spectacular underwater light shows of bioluminescence.

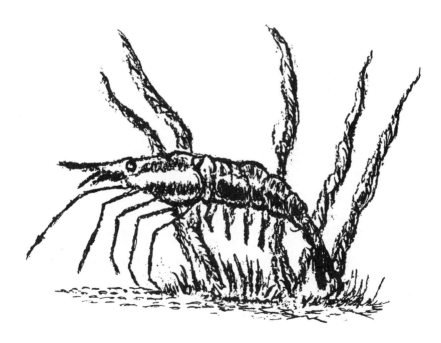

Sewing shrimp (*Alpheus pachychirus*) create their own living chambers by stitching strands of seaweed into 10- to 12-inch tubes. They lie on their backs and pull together the threads of seaweed using their second legs, or chelates, like needles. Other shrimp, such as certain species of *Upogebia* which live on the west coast, dig elaborate burrows up to three feet deep in which to live.

Cleaner shrimp (*Stenopus hispidus*) have developed a unique way of obtaining their dinner. They pick parasites and other debris off of fish, which wait in line for this service. Loud snapping sounds are used by *Alpheus*, the snapping or pistol shrimp, to stun their food and chase away predators.

Of the many species of shrimp that exist, only a few are commonly used for human consumption. On the North Carolina coast, these are the *Penaids*, a primitive group which includes white shrimp (known in Ocracoke as greentails), pink (or spotted) shrimp, and brown shrimp. Each has a unique life cycle, which determines the way it is harvested.

Late spring and early summer nights are the best time to harvest pink or spotted shrimp, which grow big and plump while wintering in estuary creeks. White shrimp, on the other hand, are harvested by day in the fall. And brown shrimp, North Carolina's main harvest shrimp, may be available day or night from late June through October.

Shrimpers and residents at Ocracoke look forward to shrimp season, wondering if each new year will be a good one. The abundance of shrimp depends primarily on the temperature and salinity of the water as the shrimp develop. Warm temperatures and high salinity in the spring usually mean lots of shrimp in the summer and fall.

Other factors may affect the shrimp catch as well. Heavy rains, which wash pesticides into the creeks on the mainland, can kill the developing larvae, precluding a good harvest on the coast. Development of salt marshes can destroy their nurseries, and pollution of coastal waters can weaken their immune systems.

Having tried my hand at heading shrimp, I decided to see what it was like to work on a shrimp boat. I hired on as a crew member on the *Captain Elmo*, a shrimp boat owned and operated by Laurie Fulcher. We set out for Pamlico Sound at sunset. Laurie's sister, Ellen Marie, my good friend and an experienced shrimper, was along. We set the nets on the outriggers, lowered them into the water, and waited anxiously for our first haul.

The *Captain Elmo* plowed through the dark waters, the boat rocking monotonously with the gentle swells. After an hour, Laurie hauled in the nets and the first one was lowered onto the deck. I stared at the incredible mass of living creatures that squirmed on the culling tray. As I stared, I felt my stomach begin to do strange things. Ellen Marie called excitedly for me to help, but instead I found myself stretched out on the bunk in the bow of the boat, wishing that I were anywhere but on a shrimping expedition in Pamlico Sound. Laurie took pity on me and, turning *Captain Elmo* around, took me back to the dock in Silver Lake. So much for my career as a shrimper.

On the final phase of the shrimping business, however, I am quite adept—consumption. Steamed, spiced, fried, sautéed, or cooked with pasta or rice—any way you can serve shrimp—I'm an expert on them all.

The Mosquito: Ghoul on Wings
or Giver of Life?

Buzz. Ouch. Slap. Buzz. Buzz. Ouch. Slap. Buzz.

That seems to be the rhythm of existence at certain times of the year on Ocracoke and nearby islands. It is a rhythm that makes dogs whine and ponies run for shelter. It causes some people to slather themselves with Skin So Soft or Cutter's insect repellent, others to hide behind air-conditioned walls, and still others to leave the island completely.

Ocracoke's mosquitoes are infamous. T-shirts bear such slogans as "I gave blood on Ocracoke," along with ferocious-looking insect monsters on the front. Outdoor bars provide free cans of repellent for each table, knowing they would have no customers without them. Residents discuss the mosquitoes the way most folks discuss the weather.

Of course, mosquitoes are not always a problem. I can recall entire summers when I hardly suffered a bite, autumns when I sat on my deck under the stars with no Skin So Soft in sight, springtimes when I peacefully launched my kayak in the marsh without running or cursing madly. But when conditions are ripe, watch out!

Mosquitoes are actually a kind of two-winged fly belonging, as do other insects, to the phylum *Arthropoda*. They are closely related to midges, black flies, and horse flies, but are distinguished from them by scales on their wings and a long projecting proboscis, or mouthpiece. The name mosquito is derived from a Spanish word that means "little fly," referring to the slender shape. There are about 2,700 species of these obnoxious bloodsuckers, all belonging to the family *Culicidae*. Most live in the tropics, but North America hosts about 130 species.

Mosquitoes have been a nuisance to humans for eons. They tormented Caesar's troops in first century Rome and Spanish explorers in sixteenth century Mexico. D.H. Lawrence epitomizes the unpopularity of the little insect in his poem "The Mosquito," in which he addresses it as a "ghoul on wings" with an "evil little aura... obscenely ecstasied sucking live blood."

Unpopular as mosquitoes have been, however, it was not until the early 1900s that their destructiveness was fully realized. Their habit of moving from person to person, drawing and injecting blood and saliva as they go, causes the spread of disease; epidemics of malaria, yellow fever, and encephalitis can all be blamed on them. The building of the Panama Canal, during which 22,000 workers died of mosquito-borne diseases, proved how deadly mosquitoes could be. Its completion signaled a great human triumph not only over engineering difficulties, but also over malaria, yellow fever, and other mosquito-related illnesses.

At least residents and visitors to Ocracoke do not have to worry about catching diseases from mosquitoes. Even though the island's most common mosquitoes, *Anopheles* and *Culex*, are potential carriers, there are no mosquito-borne diseases in the area. People do, however, need to keep their dogs on medication to prevent deadly heartworms, which are passed on by mosquitoes.

Aggravating and irritating though they may be, mosquitoes are fascinating creatures. The Roman scholar Pliny, back in the first century, described them as "one of the wonders of nature, providing on such a small scale all the five senses and other requirements of life."

These tiny creatures weigh so little that 25,000 would be required to make an ounce. They are capable of flying 30 miles per hour, beating their wings 400 to 600 times per second. Most, though not all, species are nocturnal. Because of their propensity for causing disease, they probably are the most studied of all insects.

Mosquitoes begin their lives as eggs, which are laid individually or in rafts of several hundred in stagnant water. Some mosquitoes lay their eggs in permanent waters, such as salt marshes, and these eggs hatch in a specific number of days. Other species lay their eggs in dry hollows, such as a tree stump, and when rain fills the hollows, the eggs develop and hatch rapidly.

The eggs hatch into monstrous-looking wrigglers, larvae with bulbous heads and long transparent bodies, covered with stiff protruding hairs. These aquatic monsters spend the next two to three weeks feeding on diatoms and protozoa, floating at the surface to breathe, fleeing to the bottom to hide from predators, and growing in a series of three moults. After the third moult, they undergo a transformation and emerge as pupae. During this stage, which lasts two to three days, wings and legs develop. Then the pupae pump air into their stomachs, causing their skins to split, and emerge as soft, wet arthropods. They climb up a stem, dry off in the air, and buzz off—adult mosquitoes at last.

The blood-sucking frenzy does not begin yet, however. In fact, it never begins among the male mosquitoes, which subsist on plant nectar. The females need the high protein content of blood to produce viable eggs. They eat plant fluids until they mate, after which they use their antennae to detect the warm moist bodies of their hosts.

When they have located a victim, they insert their long, thin proboscis, which contains six stylets: two cutting blades, two sword-like needles, and two tubes. Using the blades and needles to break the surface of the skin, they withdraw blood through one tube and inject saliva through the other. It is this saliva, which contains a coagulant to prevent the blood from clotting, that causes a mosquito bite to itch.

Female mosquitoes indulge in one or more huge blood feasts, consuming two to three times their body weight. Then they rest until time to lay their eggs, a process that is repeated several times during the warm season. Most mosquitoes live for less than a month, though some females hibernate (often in houses) through the winter. Once the eggs are laid, the cycle begins again, producing another generation of those repugnant, blood-thirsty pests.

There are, however, two sides to every story, and mosquitoes are no exception. Their larvae provide an important food source for hatchling fish and shrimp, which use the marshes as a nursery ground, as well as for turtles, frogs, and water insects. Bats, swallows, spiders, and dragonflies rely on the adult mosquitoes for sustenance. Scientists speculate that only one out of every 200 mosquitoes hatched reaches maturity. This means that most of the rest become food for fish, shrimp, birds, or something else in the ecosystem. If humans were to successfully eliminate mosquitoes (a highly unlikely possibility), they might eliminate a good proportion of our fisheries and wildlife.

Many of the methods used to get rid of mosquitoes, such as draining wetlands and spraying with pesticides, have proven detrimental —sometimes devastating—to the environment. We have learned the hard way about some of the effects, and we are still learning.

Draining wetlands destroys natural water-filter systems, flood controls, and nurseries for our fisheries. Pesticides that kill mosquitoes often affect birds, frogs, dragonflies, and other creatures that would otherwise control their population naturally. Natural methods of mosquito control, such as encouraging bats, purple martins, and swallows, and cleaning up man-made pockets of stagnant water, are safer and healthier in the long run.

Blessed is the evening when you can walk down a lane in Ocracoke in shirt sleeves, wearing no smelly insect repellent, free from the rhythm of buzzing mosquitoes and slapping hands. But even more blessed is an evening soothed by the rhythm of tree frog duets, the swoosh of hunting bats, the splash of bluefish pursuing schools of killifish in the marsh. It may be that without the one, we cannot have the other.

Mosquitoes are part of the environment, a vital strand in the web of life. While they may not be a strand we humans like, they are a part many other animals depend on. I curse them, I slap them, and I pray for evenings free from their annoying buzz. In short, I hate them.

But whenever I fall into the old routine—Buzz. Ouch. Slap. Buzz —I try to remember that it is the rhythm not only of torment and aggravation, but of life on Ocracoke. I think it's worth it.

Drama at Sunset:
River Otters

A shrill cry pierced the evening air, followed by a splash. Only a circle of undulating ripples was left as we scanned the dark waters of the harbor. Within seconds, another cry, more piercing than the first, sounded from the other side of the dock. Though we studied the water carefully, both the source and the cause of the cries were a mystery.

It was early evening, and I had stopped by the Jolly Roger, an outdoor bar and restaurant overlooking Silver Lake Harbor, to watch the sunset. It was the end of a warm August day and, except for the mosquitoes, a pleasant time to be out.

Drink in hand, I walked out to the dock. As I approached the end, I noticed a group of tourists wearing curious and concerned expressions. As I drew near, I heard, above the strains of a guitar from the bar, the oddly disquieting cries.

I joined the group. Peering down into the dark water, I finally saw a small blob, which appeared to be a head. From this head I heard, once again, the poignant squeal of distress. A closer look, corroborated by one of the tourists, revealed that it was the head of an otter. As before, a cry from the other side of the dock seemed to beckon it, and the otter dove and swam in the direction of the second voice.

After a few minutes of anxious watching and talking, we concluded that they were a mother otter and her baby, who were separated from one another. They were searching desperately, but were unable to find one another in the labyrinth of docked boats. The frantic terror of the baby was obvious, as was the anxiety of the mother, but though we could see what was going on, we were unable to help.

Soon a small crowd gathered to watch the little drama unfold, and we forgot all about the spectacular sunset on the horizon.

"Are they sea otters?" someone asked. Having talked about them before with several Ocracoke natives, I was able to answer the question.

"They're river otters," I said, and went on to explain that while there are no rivers on Ocracoke, the river otters seem to flourish in the salty creeks and harbor, often helping themselves to fish and bait in the boats of local fishermen.

River otters are members of the weasel family, the *Mustelidae*. They, along with the minks, which are of the same family and also reside on the island, spend most of their lives near water. Of the two, otters are the more aquatic. Known by the scientific name of *Lutra canadensis*, they are close cousins of the larger sea otters that live on the Pacific coast of North America as well as in Europe and Asia.

They have long, muscular bodies with broad, flattened heads, tapering tails, and thick, dark brown fur coats (paler in coastal otters, such as these). Special adaptations, such as webbed feet and dense waterproof pelts, enable them to swim and live in the water. Their high metabolic rates help keep them warm. High levels of oxygen in their blood enable them to remain under water in long dives, and large-capacity lungs provide buoyancy in the water.

In order to see underwater and pursue fish, their main diet, otters have modified, spherical lenses in their eyes. These act something like the goggles used by scuba divers. In waters that are too dark to see the fish, otters use their whiskers, or vibrissae, to detect the motion of their prey.

Besides fish, river otters eat mussels, crayfish, crabs, frogs, and an occasional bird or muskrat. On Ocracoke, where they live close to humans, some of them have developed the habit of investigating fishing boats during the night, helping themselves to any morsels left behind by the fishermen.

Otters are basically shy and stay away from humans. As a result, they seldom show themselves except at night. The family we were watching probably never would have allowed us to see them had they not been in trouble.

The baby we were hearing was most likely about four months old. River otters normally give birth in late spring. Litters usually contain two to three cubs, born completely blind and helpless. They mature in about two years.

The Iroquois Indians believed that otters and other water mammals had an influence on the health and fortunes of humans. The Otter Society, composed of Iroquois women, gave thanks to the otters and, in a water-sprinkling ceremony, asked their help in curing people who were ill.

Otter pelts were one of the principal items sought in the early fur trade that opened this country to colonization. Pacific sea otters were the primary victims of this trade and were brought to the point of extinction early in this century. River otters also were trapped and, in parts of the United States, even completely eradicated.

Now considered cute and likeable, otters were previously regarded as pests, particularly in Europe. Bounties were placed on them, and otter hounds were bred and used to exterminate them. Later, otter hunting came to be considered a sport, similar to fox hunting. River otters are extinct now in a number of European countries, and are protected by law in others. Today, loss of habitat is the main reason for the decline of river otters. Much of eastern North Carolina still has a healthy population, however.

As darkness settled, it became more difficult to see the separated otters, but their cries of distress continued to resound, each time from a different place. It seemed that mother and cub would never find one another.

The evening had a happy ending, however. Amidst grunts and soft mews, the family was reunited and happily disappeared into the darkness. Brought together by our concern for the otters, my new friends and I returned to the Jolly Roger to enjoy the music, feeling relieved and privileged to have observed the little drama.

A Tale of Two Dolphins

It was a beautiful, late summer day as the two bottlenose dolphins leaped and dove in the silver waters off Ocracoke's north end. The fish were plentiful, and the feeding was good. Traveling slowly along the Atlantic coast, they found this a good place to spend a few days.

Meanwhile, far to the south, a mass of violent winds swirled, danced and gradually moved northeast. Declared a hurricane by weather watchers, the storm appeared to be on a collision course with the Outer Banks. As it worked its way up the coast, it gained strength, carrying with it a promise of disaster.

While the dolphins frolicked in the surf at the northern end of the island, at Ocracoke village, we humans were busy preparing for the storm. Warned by the weather forecasts, we knew we had only a day or so to get ready.

Most of the tourists lined up to take one of the ferries off the island, but a number of residents planned to stay and ride out the turbulence. We boarded up windows, brought in lawn chairs and potted plants, and stocked up on candles and flashlight batteries. Fishermen put extra lines on their boats, and I brought my canoe out of the creek, tying it to one of the timbers under the house. The men in the Coast Guard and the rangers who managed the National Seashore prepared to answer the many emergencies that might arise.

By evening, the dolphins could sense that something was astir in the weather, but they did not know that there was a hurricane heading for Ocracoke. They spent a restless night as the winds picked up and the waves grew larger. The next day, the winds began to blow in earnest, and ominous clouds drifted across the horizon. The surf near the shore grew wild, white-capping in great fountains which sprayed across the cold, gray ocean swells. The dolphins were growing nervous, but they stayed close to the island. The rain began. The wind howled. The waters began to rise.

Back in the village, it was growing dark. People found a high piece of ground on which to park their cars, and a warm, dry room in which to wait out the storm. A few hardy souls braved the pounding rain and gusting winds to stop at the pub for a beer or to drive out to the water's edge and watch the storm. But as the waters rose in the streets, most of us shed our rain gear and rubber boots and went inside. The electricity went out, and the village was swathed in darkness as the storm pounded around it.

The dolphins, frightened now, sought a quiet place under the ocean's surface to escape the hurricane. In the deep water, it was relatively still, and they felt safe, but they knew that they would soon have to come up for air. As they fought their way to the surface, the waves tossed them about and crashed down upon them. They lost control, and it became useless to try to swim. They felt themselves being lifted and carried on a great swell toward the shore.

It was shallow now, too shallow. The waters had carried the dolphins up onto the narrow strip of sand that was Ocracoke Island. The giant waves pushed and dragged them toward Pamlico Sound on the other side. One of the dolphins reached deeper water. Still tossed by the waves, it managed to right itself and swim into the sound. It turned around, looking for its friend, but the other dolphin was nowhere to be found. The first dolphin searched frantically, to no avail.

The second dolphin had not been so lucky. The waters receded, leaving it stranded in the marsh on the edge of the sound. It struggled, more frightened than ever before, for it knew that beaching meant almost certain death. It heard the shrill lonely cry of its friend but was unable to answer. The waves continued to break over it, but no more giant swells came to wash it back into the sea.

Morning arrived, and the people in the village came out to look at the damage. The wind had died down, the rain had stopped, and the sky was clearing. The eye of the hurricane had missed us—we were lucky this time. We pulled the boards off the windows and began putting things back to normal. Park Service rangers drove along the seashore beach, looking for people or animals in need of help. But no one thought to look in a remote marsh at the north end of the island.

Three days passed. The weather returned to normal and visitors began returning to Ocracoke. A lawyer from the mainland came with his family to enjoy the quiet after the storm. He decided to take his family flounder gigging in the shallows of the sound one evening. As they waded in the knee-deep water, one of them spied an odd shape near the shore. They went to investigate. It was a dolphin, partially submerged in the mud and the marsh grass. A closer look showed that it was still alive.

The lawyer reported the beached dolphin to Wayne Elliot at the National Park Service, who contacted the Coast Guard and David Fletcher of North Carolina Marine Fisheries. Traveling by jet ski and bringing along an army cot to use as a stretcher, they all converged on the marsh where the dolphin was stranded.

They found it weak. About a third of its body was badly blistered by the sun. They applied Vaseline and aloe gel to the burns. The dolphin seemed to know that they were there to help, and lay quietly as they worked.

David Fletcher and Wayne Elliot talked as they applied the gel. They explained that the animal's chances of survival were not good. Dolphins, which are a kind of small, toothed whale, cannot live on land. Although they evolved from land mammals and share many characteristics with them, they have made the water their home for 50 to 60 million years. They have adapted to life in the sea, and their skeletal frames cannot support their weight on land for long. Neither can their skin survive the dry air and hot sun.

This was a bottlenose dolphin, sometimes mistakenly called a porpoise. The bottlenose is the type of dolphin most often seen cavorting in the waves off the coast of North Carolina. It has a streamlined body that is gray to brown in color, with a lighter-shaded belly. Its distinctive beak gives it its name. It grows to about nine feet in length and may live for up to 40 years. The male is larger than the female.

Bottlenose dolphins usually travel in pods, or small groups, and males often form close bonds with one another. Highly intelligent, they talk to each other by means of whistles or squeals produced by forcing air through their blow holes. They use a unique method of navigation, known as echolocation, which is similar to sonar. They also use this method to locate schools of fish, which, along with assorted invertebrates, compose their diet. Celebrated in history and mythology, these dolphins show a special fondness for human beings, and there are many reports of them saving sailors' lives.

Now David, Wayne, and the others would do what they could to save the dolphin. They lifted it onto the cot, where it lay still as they carried it across the marsh and shallow flats to deeper water. They laid it gently in the sound, where it struggled to right itself. As the rescuers watched, they saw a movement close by. Another dolphin, shining silver in the sunlight, leaped from the water and performed a flip in mid-air! The weakened dolphin, encouraged, swam to its friend. They were reunited again.

The pair of dolphins remained in a protected cove near the inlet for about two weeks, apparently to give the beached one a chance to recuperate. David Fletcher told me the story of the rescue the next day, so I, along with him and the rangers, checked often to make sure they were doing all right. The weak one seemed to be recovering and gaining strength.

Then one day, they were gone. They had returned at last to their home in the ocean. Perhaps, if you stand on the beach at Ocracoke on a clear day and look toward the horizon, you will see them frolicking in the waves, together again.

An Odyssey Begins:
Loggerhead Turtle Hatching

We left the village at 6:30 a.m., just as the sun was beginning to creep toward the horizon. Three of us squeezed into the front of the National Park Service pickup truck: Marty Harris, Rebecca Bruten, and myself.

With Marty at the wheel, we headed toward the far end of the island. As the eastern sky turned from gray to pale yellow, Marty slowed the pickup and turned onto a sandy access road toward the ocean. Between the dunes, he stopped briefly to set the four-wheel drive, then accelerated as we plunged through the deep sand and onto the hard, damp surface of the beach.

As we headed southward, Rebecca and I scanned the dunes, watching for the markers, but Marty spied the first one. He stopped the truck and we all got out to look. We saw nothing except windswept, water-hardened sand. Three times we did this. At the fourth marker, Marty, who was ahead of Rebecca and me, motioned excitedly for us to hurry. The marker was surrounded by what looked like miniature bulldozer tracks, all headed toward the ocean.

This is what we had come to find. The tracks indicated that a loggerhead turtle nest had hatched during the night. Our jobs as National Park Service volunteers was to check the nest and make sure that all the hatchlings made it safely to their future home, the Atlantic Ocean.

Two months earlier, volunteers had patrolled the beach searching for loggerhead nests. Fourteen had been found. Most were marked and left in place. A few, however, were in areas subject to flooding or heavy traffic, so they were carefully moved to safer sites.

Loggerhead eggs are incubated by the warmth of the sand and their own embryonic heat. The hatching process usually takes about three days. During this time, the tiny reptiles crawl around underground, breathing the oxygen in the nest. Finally, one night, a single hatchling bursts through to the surface, and the rest follow in a great odyssey to the sea.

Many perils await tiny loggerheads. There had been concern that the hurricane we'd had earlier in the summer might have drowned the nests that had been marked, or might have packed the sand too thick and hard for the baby turtles to dig out. The many tracks we saw at this nest were clear evidence that it had remained safe.

After digging out of the nest, the next challenge for the hatchlings is to find their way to the ocean. Scientists believe that natural light reflecting off the water serves as a guide, showing them which way to go. Human-made lights from houses, automobiles, or even flashlights, can confuse them, causing them to turn away from the water and become stranded. But all of the tracks at this nest led in the right direction.

Even finding the right direction is no assurance of safety. Other obstacles and enemies must be contended with. A tire track can be an insurmountable barrier for the tiny turtles, which are only two to three inches long. If they are still out at daybreak, gulls might swoop down and seize them. But darkness is no assurance of safe passage.

Ghost crabs lurk in their holes, waiting to attack, and the sad story of one such encounter was written in the sand at this nest. Tracks showed where a baby loggerhead had struggled for its life against a ghost crab before being dragged into its hole.

We saw no signs of lost or struggling turtles, and the tracks suggested that most of the young ones had made it to the water. But when Marty dug down into the nest to make sure that all of the turtles had escaped, he found that three had not made it out. He gave them a helping hand, and they immediately began their trek to the ocean.

We followed, helping them over tire tracks and around ghost crab holes. Two hurtled forward at incredible speed, allowing nothing to deter them. They plunged into the water, where they would have to evade hungry fish and other predators and stay away from fish nets on their journey to the Gulf Stream.

The last turtle was slower. It struggled valiantly toward the ocean. After getting there, it repeatedly swam out, only to be washed back by the waves. Finally, however, the surf swept it up and carried it out.

We cheered. We knew that only one in 1,000 hatchlings survived to adulthood. The odds were that none in this nest would make it, but perhaps this would be that special one.

Fall

At the Mercy of the Wind

The surface of the bay was a glistening mirror, reflecting azure sky and lace-tipped clouds, as I sat on *Aurora*, a 28-foot sailing sloop. The snow-white sail above my head flapped lazily back and forth as a puff of wind caressed it now and then, but otherwise, it was motionless. My friend Don Stein, the captain, had a bored, somewhat frustrated expression on his face as he studied a crossword puzzle. We were sitting perfectly still, otherwise known as "becalmed."

Far different was our trip across Pamlico Sound a few weeks before. On that brisk afternoon, our sails were barely hoisted up the mast at Ocracoke before the wind seized them and sent us flying out of Silver Lake Harbor. The jenny, or foresail, resembled a silver albatross, leading us through the channel with the mainsail billowing out behind.

Aurora listed to starboard, pushed so far into the water by the force of the wind that waves splashed against the portholes. Water sprayed across the bow, soaking us each time the sloop dipped into an ominous trough. We must have been a sight to behold.

Unfortunately, I did not have the pleasure of a spectator's view to enjoy the beauty of our graceful flight. From where I sat at the stern, I was only aware of the constant undulating motion as *Aurora* pitched and tossed. Up-and-down, up-and-down, with the inexorable wind pushing us onward. Before long, I was stretched out in the cabin, utterly incapacitated, seasick.

Fall

Since that first day of our voyage, when we sailed from Ocracoke across Pamlico Sound to Belhaven, heading north through the inland waterway to the Chesapeake Bay, I had become very familiar with the capriciousness of the wind. Living on a sailboat, I found myself totally at its mercy, both its beneficiary and its victim.

It had given us glorious days of smooth sailing—a wonderfully clean, quiet, free source of energy to power our boat. It had stubbornly insisted on blowing in the opposite direction of where we wanted to go, so that we had to tack continuously back and forth to make a passage. It had kept us awake through long nights, tossing the boat about, tugging at the anchor, while thunder and lightning cavorted around us. It had refused to blow at all, leaving us becalmed as we were now.

One day as we approached Elizabeth City, moving along at about four knots, the wind died and we found ourselves sitting still, only a few miles from our destination. The captain, in a moment of impatience, said a prayer to the Wind God: "Blow, wind, blow!"

Magically, the wind picked up, blowing from the stern. We were able to hoist the spinnaker, a lovely little sail that resembles a parachute, and make a perfect run up the Pasquotank River.

But the wind did not stop. Harder and harder it blew, until there were whitecaps flashing around us and an ominous wailing in our ears. As we approached the dock, we pulled down the sails, but so powerful was the wind that it continued to push us forward, driving *Aurora's* bow toward the concrete. I was not strong enough to stop us, and the bowsprit was splintered like a toothpick. Don will think twice now before he prays for wind again!

Curious about the invisible force that had so influenced our sailing trip, I asked Don what caused the wind and its whimsical behavior. He explained that there were many forces that affected its actions. He referred me to a book, *Weather for the Mariner*, where I learned how complex and unpredictable the dynamics of wind can be.

Wind, which is simply air in motion, is indeed the result of many interacting forces. The rotation of the earth, temperature changes, the tidal pull of the moon and sun, seismic disturbances such as earthquakes, and the curvature and topography of the earth all affect its behavior. As the earth rotates on its axis and revolves around the sun, different areas are warmed or cooled, both by seasons and by day and night. Warm air, which is lighter than cold air and less dense, rises. Cold air pushes its way under it and creates pressure. Air near the earth's surface moves from areas of high pressure to areas of low pressure. This creates air circulation, or wind.

Some winds, such as the trade winds, are steady and dependable. Others are sporadic and dangerous.

High pressure systems (with winds moving clockwise in the northern hemisphere) typically mean good weather, with light winds. Low pressure systems (with counter-clockwise movement) bring storms with strong, sporadic winds. A hurricane can be the result of a continually spiraling low pressure system.

Long before meteorologists began studying weather, people around the world were trying to explain the wind. In Polynesian mythology, Rake, the god of wind, and his wind children blow through holes at the edge of the horizon. The Iroquois god Gash was believed to hold the winds in a mountain cave, the "home of the winds." The Algonquins recognized the different characteristics of the winds by naming them. The east wind was Wabun, or Morning Bringer; the west was Kabeyun, Father of the Winds; the north was Kibibonokko, the Fierce One; and the south was Shawondasse, the Lazy Wind.

In India, it was said that the wind was made up of ghosts who had died of the fever. In some Eskimo tribes, the "House of Winds" was the place where the spirits of the dead gathered.

In Greek mythology, the warden of the winds was Aeolus, the son of Poseidon. He kept the winds chained in a cave. One day, he gave the winds to Odysseus in an oxhide sack. When his crew opened the sacks, the winds escaped and swept the ship away, leaving only Odysseus to return.

We had been lucky on our sailing trip, with mostly sunny skies and good weather. We had opened no forbidden sacks, and had returned home relatively unscathed.

But back at Ocracoke, we still need to understand the wind. For like a sailboat, an island is at the mercy of the wind. When a nor'easter blows, the ferries may stop running and the electricity may go out, leaving us stranded and using lantern light. In late summer, the wind may blow and swirl into a hurricane, drive tourists away, and cause islanders to "batten the hatches." A brisk sea breeze can blow the mosquitoes and green-heads away, leaving the island free of those annoying buzzing sounds and stings, and allowing us to sit in the yard at night without wearing smelly repellent. And the right wind can produce a perfect "curl" for surfers, meaning that a good number of folks won't make it to work, but can be found silhouetted against the sky atop their sculpted boards—or tumbling beneath a wave.

The wind affects the fisherman's catch—how many fish, what kinds, and where they are. It can prevent a waterman from being able to get out to check his nets, and a strong gale can mean that when he does go out, the nets are no longer there.

The wind at Ocracoke determines the success of the kayaking and windsurfing businesses. It makes the ponies nervous and too jumpy to ride. If it blows on a high tide and a full moon, the streets may fill up with water so that you can't drive your car. Living on an island, like living on a sailboat, means living with the wind.

Scientists write about the dynamics of air circulation; weathermen try to predict upcoming gales; fishermen study the way a "blow" will affect the fishing; sailors attempt to harness its power to sail across the seas. But does anyone, I wonder, really understand the magic, the spirit, and the mystery of the wind? I am reminded of the poem Robert Louis Stevenson wrote more than a hundred years ago:

O you that are so strong and cold,
O blower, are you young or old?
Are you a beast of field and tree,
Or just a stronger child than me?
O wind, a-blowing all day long,
O wind, that sings so loud a song!

Sapphires in the Sea:
Bioluminescence

Summer was over, the crowds of tourists had left the island, and we were heading back to Ocracoke, looking forward to settling in for a long, quiet winter. We had been sailing the Chesapeake Bay in *Aurora*.

Coming home, we had sailed "outside" through the ocean from Virginia Beach to Nags Head, coming "inside" the sounds at Oregon Inlet that morning. It had been blowing hard all day, making it tricky to tack through the meandering channel without an engine.

But once we were in the Pamlico, it was a fast, easy sail, and the weather radio kept predicting that the winds would soon lay down to an easy 10 to 15. We had hoped to reach Bigfoot Slough at daybreak, running down the channel on a good north wind and arriving at Silver Lake Harbor in time for a hot breakfast at the Pony Island Restaurant.

"Ten to fifteen," the weather station on the radio kept announcing, but as evening approached, the winds were still blowing hard. It became apparent, as the boat dipped and heeled, that cooking a hot meal was out of the question so, leaving Don at the helm, I went below for a nap.

I awakened to the sound of my name, barely audible above the shrieking of the wind and the pounding of the waves. "Pat! Take the helm!" Don shouted. "I'm going to take down the jib!" I struggled up on deck, holding on as *Aurora* heeled far to the right. It was pitch dark now, and the winds had certainly not died down out here. They were blowing a good 25 to 30 miles per hour.

I grabbed the tiller as Don made his way up front, clinging to the stays with one hand, untying the lines of the jib sail with the other. I tried hard to hear his commands over the whining of the rigging. "Release the sheet! Come about now!" I prayed that I would not make some grave error that would toss the captain into the briny stew around us. As I fought with the tiller, trying to hold a straight course, I noticed that the jib sheet line had fallen into the water. I reached quickly to pull it in.

As I hauled it back over the side, I was amazed to find myself holding in my hands what looked like a giant string of brilliant green sapphires, precious jewels plundered from the hoards of some mermaid queen. For a few seconds, they shimmered with an unearthly light, then faded into darkness. I stared, momentarily stunned by the beauty, forgetting the expediency of our precarious situation. Don's voice brought me back to reality, however, and I dropped the line and grabbed the helm, steadying *Aurora* on her course.

Don finished tying down the sail. We dropped anchor, and spent a rough, sleepless, but safe night, tossing about. Finally, as the sun came up, King Neptune tuned into the weather forecast and, laying his hand upon the waters, gentled the seas. It was a calm, beautiful day as we reached Ocracoke that afternoon, the winds perfect for a straight run down the channel and into the harbor. We missed breakfast, but we were in time for a good, hot lunch and a long rest.

As I sat relaxing in the cockpit, I thought about the evening before. It hardly seemed real now, particularly that incredible string of sapphires I had pulled out of the sea. I realized, of course, what they were. I had been looking at bioluminescent protozoans, most likely dinoflagellates, which had attached themselves to the rope when it fell into the water. The lights had been activated by the turbulent water and the darkness of the night.

Fall

I had seen them many times before, flickering in the wake of the boat on a midnight sail, flashing in the ocean surf on a summer evening at Ocracoke. I knew that they were among the most prolific life forms in the sea, one-celled plants and animals that floated with the currents and formed the base of the ocean's food chain. Individually, they were invisible to the naked eye. It was only when "turned on" by darkness and turbulence that their eerie light revealed their presence to human eyes.

The light itself is produced by special organs which release luciferin, a complex protein which acts as a fuel in the presence of the enzyme luciferase. Like other fires, it can not burn without oxygen. But unlike most fires, which release more than 90 percent of their energy as heat, the bioluminescent fires lose less than 5 percent of their energy as heat, making them an incredibly efficient light source.

Many kinds of marine life produce bioluminescence. These include a number of jellyfish, such as the comb jelly, which glows blue, and the sea walnut, which emits a green light. More than half of the species of fish and other animals that live far down in the ocean's depths produce their own light.

This same bioluminescence, or phosphorescence, as it is sometimes called, is what we see flashing through the air on summer evenings. Fireflies, also known as lightning bugs, use this light in their courtship rituals. They have special light-producing organs in their abdomens which, like the protozoans in the sea, burn luciferin.

Scientists are not sure what purpose bioluminescence serves. Some speculate that it is a protective device, scaring predators away. Others believe that it may be used by larger organisms to lure prey in. For some, it may provide light needed to fulfill their daily functions, while for others, it seems to serve no purpose at all. Apparently, the lights switch on only at night, and only, in the case of the protozoans, in the presence of some kind of disturbance.

As I thought about it, it occurred to me that the protozoans were around me in the water all the time, but it was only in the midst of a frightening storm that I could see their beauty. How much like life, I realized. A myrtle warbler singing in a shrub, a scallop shell lying on the shore, an oak leaf clinging to a branch: they are all exquisite jewels, there for everyone to share and enjoy. But we often look at them with unseeing eyes, unable to appreciate their beauty, longing instead for some nebulous dream which remains just out of reach.

No queen of Egypt or England ever possessed a necklace of jewels equal to that which I held briefly in my hands that night. It could never be bought for money, but for a fleeting moment it was mine— not to own, show off, or exploit, but to remind me of the wealth and beauty that surround us, if only see we would learn to see them.

Sea Squirts:
The Road Not Taken

Heralded by apprehensive weathermen and overly dramatic television reporters, the hurricane had whirled past Ocracoke, tossing and tumbling the cedar tree branches, agitating the sea into a caldron of angry waves, and filling the streets with sound water, before passing on up the coast.

After it had gone, residents emerged to find that little damage had been done. With few repairs to make and even fewer tourists left on the island, many locals visited the beach to see what curiosities the storm had left behind.

My friend, Kathleen O'Neal, and I decided to drive to the north end of the island. We hiked across the ramp, past the dunes, onto the hard, damp beach sand now free of storm tide. There were a few shells, a scattering of translucent, sometimes colorful jellyfish, and here and there, a gray blob resembling a slab of blubber. When I touched one of these blobs with my toe, it moved. After examining it more closely, we confirmed that the odd-looking creature, equipped with two openings that looked like spouts, was indeed alive. It spewed water at me from one of the spouts.

That, I later learned, is how it got its name, for the strange little animal was a sea squirt. Many a child has engaged in battles using this odd creature as a water gun. Also known as a sea grape or Ascidian, it belongs to the Tunicate class. Sea squirts normally are found attached to pilings, submerged lines, or other stationary objects, often in the company of barnacles. The ones on the beach this day had been wrenched loose by the powerful waves of the storm and tossed onto the shore.

The sea squirt I held in my hand was the size of a lemon, with a brownish-green translucent surface, or "tunic," that was smooth but tough. It had a globular shape and, with its two spouts, it resembled a little tea kettle. At first glance, it appeared to be a primitive, dull organism.

The truth, however, is that sea squirts and other tunicates are among the most highly evolved animals in the sea. They are members of the phylum *Chordata*, along with fish, birds, and other vertebrates (including humans.) In their infantile stage, they possess a notochord (a primitive backbone), a dorsal nerve chord (a spinal cord), and a primitive brain. They resemble tadpoles and can swim, perceive shapes with a huge, single eye, and breathe like a fish.

But instead of continuing to develop, as do tadpoles, the young sea squirts come to an abrupt halt and go into reverse. Award-winning

naturalist Gilbert Klingel calls them "the animals that grow backwards."

Using an adhesive organ located on their heads, sea squirts grasp hold of a stationary object and attach themselves to it, becoming what are known as "sessile" organisms. Their tails are absorbed, their body shapes alter, their stomachs and hearts migrate to the bottom, and their mouths enlarge into spout-like openings. One of the spouts sucks water into a basket-like filter, which strains edible organisms into the stomach. The lower spout then ejects the clean, filtered water. The walls of the filter serve as a gill for breathing, and a throbbing capsule-like heart, capable of reversing directions, pumps oxygen to hundreds of minute blood vessels. Hermaphroditic, they are often found living in clumps, resembling sea grapes—their other common name.

Some tunicates, such as the star tunicates, are colonial. They share certain functions and operate as one organism. Though seldom noticed, the tunicates are among the most abundant of marine organisms.

After learning about them, I couldn't help wondering what evolutionary fluke led to the strange backward development of the tunicates. Hundreds of millions of years ago, according to scientists, certain tunicate ancestors took the path that eventually led to today's fish, reptiles, birds, mammals, and humans. Others, already well on their way upward on the evolutionary scale, turned back for no obvious reason.

Pondering the explanation for this, I thought about the end result of the two separate paths. Tunicates lead peaceful lives, harming no other creatures. They filter the water they inhale, cleaning it and thus improving their environment. They provide homes and protection for small animals that take cover inside their basket-like bodies. Many live in commune-like colonies, sharing their functions for the benefit of all. They live in complete harmony with the world around them.

Humans, the final stage of that other evolutionary path, "the road not taken" by the tunicates, often lead violent lives, engaging in war and murder. They pollute the world around them, destroying the homes and lives of other creatures. Locked within air-conditioned walls and a facade of self-satisfaction, most have lost touch with the natural world, and live their lives in disharmony with it.

Did some of those young, free-swimming tunicates, back in the distant reaches of time, have a premonition of what was to come?

Did they somehow perceive, with senses long lost to us, that the evolutionary path they were on would lead to stress and sorrow, possibly even the destruction of the earth? Seeing this, did they simply say, "No, we won't go," and choose to retreat to a more peaceful, harmonious way of life? If so, perhaps we need to consider the choice our little cousins made so many years ago. After all, it's not too late for us to say the same thing.

Barnacles:
The Bane of the Seas

"A little shrimp-like animal standing on its head in a limestone house and kicking food into its mouth." That's how nineteenth century naturalist Louis Agassiz described the hard, shell-like mound I held in my hand. It looked like some kind of mollusk—a limpet, perhaps. And it was, in fact, believed for a long time to be a member of the phylum *Mollusca*.

Actually, it is a relative of the crab and shrimp, those lively and delicious creatures so avidly sought by fishermen and seafood lovers. No one sought out this odd little crustacean, however. In fact, it is considered to be the bane of the seas.

This was an acorn barnacle, rudely evicted from its home on the bottom of my canoe. A fierce autumn storm had forced me, with the help of a couple friends, to pull my canoe out of the creek where I had kept it for the past three months. Amidst angry wind and rain, we had hauled it over the sea wall, across Oyster Creek Road, and under an old house. Turning it upside down, I was amazed to see what looked like an entire city of miniature gray igloos anchored to the bottom.

One of my friends, a seasoned fisherman, referred to it as fouling material and, using a board, scraped most of the growth off. He advised me that, before returning the canoe to the water, I should clean it off completely.

Now I sat under the house on my up-ended canoe, wind shrieking fiercely around me, studying one of the barnacles.

I knew, of course, that barnacles attached themselves to ship keels and dock pilings, causing untold problems for the owners. But I had no idea that in just three months they could so completely take over the bottom of my canoe.

I could understand why these creatures are such a nuisance. Numbering as many as a thousand per square yard, they can reduce the speed of a ship by 50 percent, causing spoiled cargo, missed deadlines, increased fuel expenditures, and lost money. Barnacles have no doubt altered the course of human history, preventing battleships from arriving at strategic battles in time, and causing vessels racing against storms to lose the race and be battered to pieces on rocky shores. It is estimated that barnacles cause more than a billion dollars in damage each year and, according to Robert Hendrickson's *Ocean Almanac*, they "wreak more destruction for their size than any other creature in the sea."

Still, I couldn't help but feel sorry for the little guy I held in my hand. It was alive now, tightly locked within the palisade of calcareous plates that protect it and allow it to survive when out of the water at low tide. It would not survive for long, though, removed from the liquid world in which it breathes, feeds, and reproduces.

Barnacles begin their lives like other members of the class Crustacea. They emerge from eggs as free-swimming, mobile nauplius larvae and go through a series of moults, metamorphosing into shrimp-like cirripeds.

At this stage, they locate a suitable hard surface and, using a cement which is secreted by glands on their antennae, anchor themselves to their new home. From now on, they are sessile creatures, never moving again, and bearing little resemblance to their mobile cousins. Their eyes and other sensory organs disappear; they secrete a highly modified carapace in the form of six calcium carbonate plates, and their six legs turn into feather-like fans, or "cirri," which they use to push plankton into their mouths.

Barnacles usually live in large communities, necessary for successful reproduction. They are hermaphrodites, which means each animal contains both male and female organs, but they do not fertilize themselves. They have a specialized cirrus with which they pass sperm to their neighbors. Eggs are incubated within the plates until they hatch.

The little creature in my hand, barricaded within its fortress, seemed harmless enough. It was neither aggressive nor cruel, and played an important role in the marine ecosystem as it filtered water and plankton through its system. Its incredible abundance is what makes it a menace. There are hundreds of species worldwide, most of them plentiful, prolific, and fond of structures made by humans. If only a use could be found for them, then the bottom of my canoe would be considered not fouling material, but farming material.

Actually, barnacles are used by a sprinkling of people around the world. I ate stewed goose barnacles at a Makaw Indian feast on the coast of Washington one summer. In Chile, large barnacles are eaten in soups and stews; in Japan, small ones are used for fertilizer. The National Institute of Dental Research is experimenting with the idea of duplicating barnacle cement to use for making dental repairs and filling cavities. It hardens in less than 15 minutes, and has a tensile strength of 5,000 pounds per square inch.

But for now, the rain was pouring down, the wind was howling, and I didn't need any dental work or fertilizer. I might as well stay where I was and finish cleaning the barnacles off my canoe. I was tempted to scoop them all up and, braving the storm, run them back to the creek. Good sense, however, got the better of me. I wasn't even sure they would survive without being anchored to their home base, my canoe.

So, trying not to think about the fascinating but luckless creatures hiding in their limestone houses, I scraped the remaining ones off my canoe and into the sand, and waited for the storm to subside so I could return home.

The Feisty Fiddler Crabs

Late one autumn afternoon, as misty rain clouds played tag with bursts of sunlight, leaving behind little wisps of rainbow, I was cruising down Oyster Creek Road on my bicycle, enjoying the wind in my hair and the fine spray on my face.

It was a challenge to avoid the omnivorous potholes and balance the bag of groceries between my knees. Suddenly, I slammed on my brakes, nearly capsizing the bike, the groceries, and myself. There, waving a fearsome weapon in a most threatening manner, stood *Uca pugilator*.

He held his ground as my bicycle tire squealed to a halt just inches away. As I approached, now on foot, he fearlessly raised himself up to his full height, his weapon poised for attack.

I couldn't help but laugh. The mighty warrior came no higher than my big toe, but I had to admit that I was impressed. He was fully prepared to take me on, either on or off my bicycle. What courage! I could picture him as the villain in a second-rate adventure movie: *The Invasion of the Pugilators.* And there, blown up to more than a thousand times his natural size, threatening the whole human race with his over-sized claw, would be the tiny fiddler crab before me.

I bent down and gently scooped him into my hand and carried him to the side of the road. Not one to give up easily, he struggled and tried to give my finger a pinch. I set him down and he scurried away in a great huff. I climbed back on my bicycle, situated my bag of groceries, and continued on my way. But now my curiosity was piqued, so I decided to learn more about these feisty little crabs.

Uca pugilator, the sand fiddler crab, and *Uca pugnax,* the marsh fiddler crab, derive their scientific names from the Latin word *pugnare,* which means "to fight." My close encounter with this one left no doubt that the name was earned. Their common name, "fiddler crab," comes from the resemblance of the male's large claw to a fiddle. And just as some lovesick musician might try to woo his lady with a heart-bleeding fiddle tune, the male *Uca* clicks out a musical rhythm, using his fiddle claw, to court his lady love.

If you spend much time in Ocracoke, or anywhere on an undeveloped Atlantic coastline, you are likely to encounter fiddler crabs. They are small, with a squarish brown carapace (or shell) only about an inch across. Only the males have the large fiddle claw; females have two small claws known as "spoon claws," which are used for securing food and digging burrows. The spectacular "fiddle claw" is useless except in fighting and courting.

Fiddlers begin their life, like other crustaceans, as eggs within their mothers' abdominal flaps. After about two months, they, along with about a quarter million brothers and sisters, are released into the water. There, they spend their first few days as predatory, tadpole-like zoea. They pass through several metamorphoses over a period of about three weeks, developing into megalopa. Then they finally turn into their adult crab-like forms. At this time they return to land, where they live at the water's edge.

To help adapt to life within the tidal zone, fiddlers have both gills and primitive lungs. They dig foot-long tunnels, carrying out the dirt in tiny balls attached to their legs. They pile the balls of dirt around the tunnel entrance, providing protection from sun and flooding.

In mating season, males court the females by waving their large fiddle claws and making clicking sounds. They ferociously fight off competitors and intruders. After a successful wooing, the female follows the male into his tunnel, which he then closes. After mating, the female lays her eggs and remains in the chamber, incubating the eggs under her abdominal flap until it is time for them to hatch.

Fiddlers are omnivorous, but most of their diet is composed of algae and plant matter, which they carry onto land to consume. In turn, they become dinner for birds, fish, mammals, and other crabs. During cold weather, they are inactive, staying in their tunnels below the frost line.

As I have learned more about these minute crustaceans, my respect and affection for *Uca pugilator* and its cousin, *Uca pugnax*, have increased. Someone should design a bumper sticker for me, warning tailgaters that I will do anything within reason to avoid running over one of these little spitfires. It should read, "I brake for fiddler crabs."

Return to the Wild:
The Green Heron

The little brown marsh bird did not know what was wrong, but he felt that his world was out of kilter. He was weak and disoriented, and the grasshopper leaping through the tall grass did not stir his appetite.

He ruffled the gray-green feathers on his back and drew his head in, hunkering down in the shade of a myrtle bush. The shadow of a great blue heron passing overhead did not interest him. Nor did the raucous cries of the crows fighting over a dead fish nearby. He sat still for a while, then, feeling restless, began to wander.

He found himself in unknown territory and became frightened. Too ill to fly or to try to pick his way back, he sank down, seeking shelter within the spartina grass, awaiting his fate.

A monstrous shape loomed above. His instincts told him to flee, but as he tried to run, he became tangled in the grass. He heard strange sounds; then an unknown creature seized him. He struggled briefly and froze, held captive by a human hand.

"It's a green-backed heron, a young one," I said, when I saw him a day later.

The veterinarian who was showing me the bird held it up, demonstrating that there was nothing wrong with its wings or legs. But it couldn't fly, and it wouldn't eat, he explained. The bird had been brought to him by a tourist, who had found it on the side of the road. Now he was turning it over to me, a wildlife rehabilitator, to try to revive it and return it to the wild. But looking at the little heron, I was not optimistic.

My training and experience has taught me that herons are extremely sensitive, hard to keep alive in captivity. Although it had no external injuries or signs of trauma, I knew that it never would have allowed itself to be caught unless it had some kind of serious internal disorder. It was extremely thin.

A number of possibilities flitted through my mind. Lead or mercury poisoning from industrial pollution, poisoning from pesticides or chemicals, or a variety of natural avian diseases or parasites could be the problem.

Most wild birds have parasites, so an examination revealing intestinal worms did not necessarily mean that this was the problem. But I knew that herons are particularly susceptible to heavy infestations of nematodes, which will eventually migrate throughout the body, causing emaciation, nervous system disorders, and death. I decided to treat the bird for parasites.

I took it home with me, riding the ferry from Hatteras to Ocracoke. At first, I fed it Isocal, a commercial liquid nutrient, administering it through a tube that I ran into its stomach. Later, attempting to duplicate its natural diet of fish, frogs and crustaceans, I fed it chopped fish and shrimp. Soon, it was eating on its own. I treated the parasites with a broad spectrum dewormer called Panacur. All this time, I kept the bird warm, dry, and quiet.

It was touch-and-go, as it is with many of the birds I treat. I tried to brace myself for its death, reminding myself that the odds of saving it were against me. But, as always, it was hard to remain detached, and the little heron seemed special.

The green-backed heron, or *Butorides striatus*, as it is known to ornithologists, is indeed special. It is our smallest heron, a chunky bird about 18 inches long. Adults have iridescent green feathers on their backs, with chestnut-colored undersides and white breasts. When alarmed or engaged in courtship, they raise the green-black feathers on their heads into a crest.

The bird in my care wore the brownish feathers and streaked undersides of a juvenile. I guessed that it was one to two years old.

These birds are among the few animals that make and use tools. Green-backed herons have been observed using bait to attract fish. They may catch and throw insects into the water, or they may use feathers, leaves, or sticks. If no other "lures" are available, they may whittle sticks into half-inch pieces to use. They toss the bait into a likely fishing hole and stand motionless, poised to seize an approaching fish within seconds. They may re-use the same bait, and if one fishing hole is unproductive, they may carry it to another spot. Young birds apparently practice throwing out various kinds and sizes of bait until they perfect the skill.

Green-backed herons live in many parts of the world. They are found throughout the United States, inland as well as on the coast. They nest throughout most of their range, laying three to six eggs on a frail platform of twigs in small trees near the water. Like other herons, they are wading birds, but they also spend a fair amount of time perching in low-growing trees.

I cared for the bird for a week. It gained weight and grew lively and active. One day, I took it out to the marsh. It stalked an insect and flew a short distance, but it was still too weak to survive on its own.

A few days later, however, I carried it in its cage to a little oasis I had found beside a winding creek where juniper trees and spartina grasses grew. Other herons were nearby.

As I carried my patient through the brush toward its new home, it paced its cage, rubbing its beak against the metal in anticipation. I set the cage down beneath the tree and opened the door. The little bird hurled itself through the door, spread its wings, and flew into a tree. It preened its feathers and examined its surroundings. It hopped from branch to branch, flew into the grass and back to the tree.

As I sat watching, I found myself wishing that I could trade places with the heron. Its new home seemed idyllic. The rustling grass and the gently swaying branches made soft music with the rhythm of the creek. The voices of tree frogs and the deep throaty cry of a great blue heron completed the sonata.

I closed my eyes, wishing that I could remain in this enchanted, emerald haven, instead of returning to the confinement of four walls and daily chores. I craved the freedom I had just bestowed upon my temporary ward.

Suddenly, I found myself caught in fantasy. I was the heron, leaping through the branches, peering out through the leaves at a dragonfly. I allowed myself the moment of ecstasy. But as the sun began to drop toward the horizon and I reluctantly began to shake myself back into reality, I realized that the fantasy was real.

In setting the little bird free, I had freed myself. I knew that when I left, a part of me would remain in the marsh, and part of the marsh would go home with me. The moment was brief, but it more than repaid all the time and effort I had devoted to saving the heron.

An Island Tradition: Yaupon

"This looks like a good one," my friend Don Stein said, nodding toward a small evergreen tree.

We were strolling along a sandy path on a little piece of high ground interlaced with the branches of juniper, wax myrtle, and yaupon. Sinuous vines of wild grape and catbrier draped the trees. The circular leaves of pennywort sprinkled the ground, looking like lime-colored coins tossed out of a pirate's chest. Meandering through this semi-tropical jungle, we would stop whenever we found a likely tree.

Now we reached up into the branches and stripped handfuls of dark green, leathery leaves into a paper bag. We tried not to take too many from any one branch, so as not to damage the tree. With enough in our bag, we hiked back along the trail and climbed into my pickup truck.

Back at my house, we spread the leaves out on a cookie sheet and put them in the oven. We baked them at 200 degrees for an hour or so, then let them cool. We repeated this over several days until the leaves were brown and crisp. Then we packed most of them into a large jar, saving out a handful.

Now for the next step. We put the handful of leaves into a pot of water with a sprinkle of cinnamon, boiled it for about 20 minutes, and *voilà!* It was ready—that famed and oft-used tonic from Ocracoke's past, yaupon tea.

Our experiment was a new one for us, but it was a continuation of a tradition that dates back to prehistoric times. Long before Europeans touched the shores of the Outer Banks, native Algonquian and Siouan Indians harvested and used the leaves of the yaupon tree. They used the tea, made from green leaves, as a purgative, to cleanse their bodies for medicinal or religious purposes. Later, European settlers, introduced to yaupon tea by the Indians, brewed it for their own enjoyment and health. They dried and baked the leaves, which removed their emetic qualities, and developed an extensive market for the product. Old-time Outer Bankers remember enjoying the drink when they were young, but in recent years it has been replaced by Lipton and other more easily obtainable drinks.

This would be our first taste of the famous tea.

The yaupon is actually a kind of holly tree, tough and hardy enough to grow in the sandy soil and survive the wind and salt spray of island storms. Known to scientists as *Ilex vomitoria* because of its early use as a purgative, the yaupon is an important component of the endangered maritime forest. It has tiny, white, four-petaled flowers between March and May. Red berries, an important food source for a variety of birds, develop between October and December.

The yaupon tree was first described in writing by John Lawson, an early English explorer and Surveyor General in North Carolina. In his book, *A New Voyage To Carolina*, he commented on the "famous yaupon," calling it a "bush that grows chiefly on the Sand-Banks and Islands; bordering on the Sea of Carolina; on this Coast is plentifully found, and in no other Place that I know of."

Lawson described the Native Americans' use of the plant for "Purging and Emeticks...drinking vast quantities of their Yaupon or Tea, and vomiting it up again, as clear as they drink it. This is a Custom amongst all those that can procure the Plant, in which manner they take it every other morning, or oftner; by which Method they keep their Stomachs clean...Besides, the great Diuretick Quality of their Tea carries off a great deal, that perhaps might prejudice their Health, by Agues, and Fevers, which all watery Countries are addicted to; for which reason, I believe, it is that the Indians are not so much addicted to that Distemper, as we are, that preventing its seizing upon them, by this Plant."

Native tribes visited the islands here to harvest yaupon leaves, often journeying from as far as 500 miles away. They bruised the leaves and twigs in a stone mortar till blackish, then smoked them over a fire. Then they spread them on mats to dry and stored them for later use. Records show that Carolina Indians not only used the tea themselves, but also sold or traded it to other tribes to the west. Yaupon played an important part in preparing for religious ceremonies, as well as in staying healthy.

Early European residents of the Outer Banks drank yaupon as a stimulant (it contains caffeine, as does Asian tea) and as a medicine. It was used as a tonic, a cure for hangovers, and as an aphrodisiac. Also known as "the black drink," yaupon tea became especially popular during the Revolutionary War and Civil War, when other tea was unavailable.

People on Ocracoke prepared and sold or traded yaupon tea for years. Ocracokers and other Bankers would chop up twigs and leaves in a chopping trough, then "seat" the yaupon in a hogshead made from a hollow log. The leaves were spread out between layers of hot rocks and left for about 36 hours. After that, they were laid out on platforms to dry, then packed in sacks or barrels.

According to Sara Ellen Gaskill, an Ocracoke native who lived on the island in the late 1800s, "a lot of people liked it…You hear them talk about it now…Daddy used to be crazy over it."

Yaupon tea was commercially produced in Frisco, a village on Hatteras Island, until the early 1900s.

But no one I knew drank the tea, and I wanted to try it.

Fall

The time had come now for the ultimate test. We poured our freshly brewed tea into mugs, added a little honey and a taste of lemon, and sat down to enjoy the moment.

"Well, not too bad..." I said. "Maybe a bit more honey and lemon...remember how healthy it is."

Actually the tea was pretty good, but I'm not ready to give up my Irish cream-flavored, home-ground coffee from Styron's Store quite yet.

Besides, the real importance of the yaupon tree is the role it plays in the ecosystem of North Carolina's barrier islands. The modest little yaupon is a part of the magic of Ocracoke.

Mysterious Journey: The Eel

I was standing on the beach at South Point, overlooking Ocracoke Inlet. It was a still day in late fall, unusual for this time of year. The blue-gray sky was flicked with foamy wisps of cirrus clouds. Across the water, I could see the low silhouette of Portsmouth Island.

The sound itself was like a looking-glass, mirroring the great dome of sky above it. Not a movement marred its gleaming surface. I knew, however, that somewhere far below that deceptive surface, a momentous event was taking place, one of the great mysteries of the sea.

The eels were passing by. I could not see them, but I knew that they were there, for this was the time, my studies had told me, for their great journey. Great hoards of them were slipping through the water, relentlessly making their way toward the distant Sargasso Sea. They had bid farewell to the rivers of North Carolina, where they had spent the last seven or more years, feeding and maturing.

Now, driven by some ancient, irresistible urge, they were returning to their birthplace. Traveling approximately 10 miles per day, fasting the entire way, they would arrive sometime in the spring. In the depths of the Sargasso Sea, 1,000 fathoms deep, they would breed, lay their eggs, and die. This was their final journey.

Eels have long been considered creatures of mystery. Although they are true fish, their resemblance to snakes gives them a different aura, and their strange migratory habits add to their mystique. Aristotle believed that eels were sexless and rose spontaneously from the "entrails of the seas." Pliny the Elder maintained that they procreated by rubbing against rocks, creating broken fragments which developed into adult eels. Early Japanese believed that eels were dragons in disguise, and many early societies considered them the reincarnations of their ancestors.

Eels have long, cylindrical bodies with dorsal, caudal, and anal fins united and extending as one long fin down their backs and up their bellies. Their scales are small; their skin is covered with mucous, which enables them to live for a long time out of water and explains the saying "slippery as an eel."

There are 30 different families of eels living throughout the world. American eels (*Anguilla rostrata*) live along the east coast of the United States from Florida to Maine. They are closely related to European eels, which make a similar but even longer journey to the same spawning grounds in the Sargasso Sea.

Different from such migratory fish as salmon, herring, and rockfish, eels are catadromous (which is Greek for down-wandering). This means that they travel from fresh water to salt water to spawn. It is necessary for them to have special water-regulating devices in order to survive in these two opposing environments.

Their life cycle was a complete mystery until this century. Adult eels seemed to simply appear out of nowhere. No larvae, or babies, could be found. Then in the early 1900s, Danish naturalist Dr. Johannes Schmidt found a young eel, or elver, as it is called, in the ocean. He searched for smaller and smaller ones, using tow nets on three boats and working his way toward the Sargasso Sea. Finally, in 1904, he found the answer to the mystery. The tiny, flat, leaf-shaped *Leptocephalus*, previously believed to be a completely different organism, was actually a newly hatched eel larva.

Dr. Schmidt learned that eels begin life as tiny eggs laid by adult females and fertilized by accommodating males. The adult eels die soon after reproducing. After a few weeks, the eggs hatch into *Lep-*

tocephalus larvae, only a quarter-inch long, which swim to the surface and spend the next few months feeding and developing. They grow into tubular, purple-eyed, transparent elvers, also known as "glass eels." These young eels soon embark on their now-famous odysseys to the continents—American eels needing a year for their journeys, European eels requiring three.

Those that survive the trip fight their way against storms and currents and travel through inlets to mainland waters. Males stay near the shore in the brackish estuaries. Females force their way upriver, climbing dam traces and even dragging themselves across land for short stretches to reach the freshwater streams and lakes that become their homes.

There they remain, scavenging for food at night, burrowing in the mud during the day. Devouring almost anything they can find, they grow into olive-brown, white-bellied adult eels up to four feet in length and weighing up to seven pounds. Then, sometime between the ages of seven and 20 years, the fully-mature fish, now known as "silver eels," answer their mysterious call and begin the long journey back through the inlets and across the ocean to their distant birthplace.

Scientists have solved the mystery of where eels go to breed, but still, no one knows how or why. What is that irresistible instinct that sets them on their course soon after birth, fighting against all odds to reach some stream or lake in North Carolina? What tells them where to go or how long to stay? And what gives them the sign that now, this particular fall, is the time to swim back to their ancient birthing and dying grounds?

Is it the pull of the tides, driven by the moon, that guides them through the deep, dark waters? Do magnetic forces emanating from the poles of the earth provide them with an unwritten map? Is it the length of day that tells them when to leave? Or some biological clock that ticks silently within them?

Whatever the answer, the force is strong and irresistible, and as I stood looking out across Ocracoke Inlet toward the beckoning sea

Fall

beyond, I felt it myself—the urge to be up and away, to seek adventure and risk death, to search for the unknown. Was longing to travel an invention of modern humankind? Or some leftover instinct from an earlier stage of our evolution, when we listened more closely to the rhythms of our bodies?

Before me, unseen, the mysterious eels were passing by. I felt it instinctively, and a strange quiver passed through me as I took one last look and turned away.

Flounder and Fishermen

A tiny pincushion of toothpicks emerged from the haze as Tom Leonard and I motored toward East Upper Rhode Shoal.

"Aim straight on it," he directed, as I steered the boat through the gentle swells.

The pincushion gradually turned into a pattern of stakes and floats. This was our destination—a pound net full, we hoped, of southern flounder.

The sun was halfway up in the eastern sky on this crisp, clear November morning as we crossed the water in the sturdy sea ox. This was the day we had been waiting for. There had been a strong northwest wind for the past two days. Not only had it blown in this beautiful morning, but it also should have brought with it the flounder that are the most important fall harvest for fishermen at Ocracoke.

I had met Tom at his house in Oyster Creek at seven, and we had sipped hot coffee as we waited for the tide to shift. He explained then that the best time to fish the nets was after a north wind. The flounder took advantage of the wind to help them in their migration to the sea, where they would spend the winter and spawn before returning to the sound. In their mass movement to the sea, some would follow the net leads, pass through the tunnels, and find themselves entrapped in the 25-foot pockets, or impoundments, that give the nets their name.

As we neared the first net, Tom took the helm and eased up slowly to release the corner lines. I was impressed by the skill required to maneuver the 19-foot boat around and through the lines and nets. He used a hand-fashioned tool, which he called a "shove-down," to hold down the net so that we could slide over it and into the impoundment. Gradually, he worked the net up onto pegs on the sides of the boat until the impoundment was reduced to a small pocket full of squirming, splashing fish.

Using a hand-held net, Tom removed several clumps of eel grass that were entwined with the fish. Then he scooped out the unwanted horseshoe crabs, puffer fish, and sting rays, and tossed them over the edge of the net to freedom. He also released a few small flatfish—hogchokers and whiffs, as well as some under-sized commercial flounder. The rest of the fish he netted into a hold in the middle of the boat. Most were southern flounder, he explained, but intermixed were a few summer flounder.

"There's a jumbo," Tom commented, depositing a nine-pound fish on the deck. "Jumbos go for two dollars a pound this week."

Commercial fishermen are paid by the pound for the fish they bring in, and the price varies from year to year and from week to week, based on the law of supply and demand. When fish are plentiful, the prices go down; when they are scarce, prices rise. Mediums were going for $1.30 a pound and large ones for $1.60 this week.

As he scooped the flounder into the hold, Tom measured the marginal ones, using a board made for the purpose. Anything over 13 inches is legal here in the sound, he noted, while 14 inches is the legal size in the ocean.

"Well, you're a lucky one," he said as he tossed a 12 ½-inch fish over the side.

He handed me a small, odd-shaped fish with brilliant green eyes.

"It's a filefish," he said. "Rub your finger over it, and you'll see why."

He tossed a couple of blowtoads, sometimes known as sea chickens, into the hold and we watched them puff up into colorful balls. "They'll be dinner, if we get enough."

When the net was empty, Tom slipped it back into the water and backed the boat out. He went around it again, ringing down the corners, before heading for the next net near Mullet Shoal. We fished three nets that morning before heading back to Ocracoke.

Also known as flukes, the flounder that lay in the boat's hold are one of the flatfish, closely related to the halibut of the west coast. They are unique in that they have flat, highly compressed bodies, swim on their side, and have both eyes on the side that faces upward. This side is normally dark and mottled; the lower side is white. Many species can change color in order to blend in with the substrate on which they are living. Some flounder are left-eyed, which means that their left side faces up and contains the eyes; others are right-eyed.

The fish Tom had caught were mostly southern flounder, a left-eyed species that spends most of its time feeding and burrowing on the bottom. This is the main species of flounder caught in pound and gill nets at Ocracoke. It is considered a healthy fishery, with numbers remaining steady from year to year.

Summer flounder, of which we had landed a few, are a similar species. They drift in the ocean and inlets as they hunt their prey and, as a result, are the primary catch of the trawl boat fishery. Summer flounder numbers have been greatly depleted in the last few years, and scientists and fishermen alike are concerned. They are experimenting with ways to restore this fishery to its former abundance.

As we motored back through the shallow sound, Tom told me to pick myself out a fish for dinner. I chose a large southern, maybe 16 inches long. I studied it as we purred along, trying to imagine what its life had been like up until this crucial point.

It would have begun life as an egg, laid in the ocean during the cold months of winter. Washed westward by tides and winds, it hatched into a larva as it gradually moved toward the sound. Originally upright and with eyes like other fish, it developed during the next 50 to 70 days into a smaller version of its present adult form. When it reached the estuary, it settled to the bottom, where it fed on shrimp, small fish, and other prey, darting across the bottom in short bursts of speed.

Growing rapidly in the estuary, it would reach a length of 12 inches in its first year. When fall came, some deeply ingrained instinct led it, along with millions of other flounder, back to the ocean. It would make this trip every year for the rest of its life, spawning in the ocean in the winter, feeding and growing in the estuaries through spring and summer. Had it not blundered into Tom's net or met some other mishap, it might have continued this pattern for eight to 12 years, reaching a length of three feet. But either fate or luck had altered its course, and now it would end up in a frying pan—prey instead of predator in the food chain that dictates life on earth.

After we eased into Silver Lake Harbor and tied up at the South Point Fish House dock, Tom shoveled the fish into baskets and handed them up to the men who worked there. They spread the fish onto a conveyer belt, where they were checked for size and packed in boxes. From there, they would be trucked to mainland restaurants and fish markets.

Tom and I headed back to Oyster Creek. My day at the pound nets was over, but for Tom and the flounder, this was a way of life: prey and predator, each involved in a daily struggle for survival. In many ways, their predicament was similar. Both depended on the sea and the sound to live. Both were threatened by the modern world, with its development and pollution, and the demands of an ever-increasing human population. For when the fish, crabs, and shrimp disappear, so will the commercial fisherman.

I was glad that, at least for now, the southern flounder were still prolific. The one I was taking home, already filleted and ready to cook, would not return to the sea. But unless human "progress" intervened, its progeny would carry on, recreating the age-old rhythm of life in the oceans.

Sea Stars:
Gangsters of the Deep

It is almost Christmas, and I am putting the finishing touches on the little juniper tree in my living room. I reach carefully through the branches and apply the last ornament—a star for the top.

This is not just any star that could be bought at a neighborhood Kmart; this star is a gift from the sea. I had found it months earlier on the north beach after a hard blow. It was no longer alive when I found it, so I took it home and dried it in the sun. Now it makes a perfect tree-top ornament, bringing a hint of the briny sea into my cozy front room.

Starfish, or sea stars, as they are more appropriately called (since they are not fish at all), are common inhabitants of our coastal waters. This one, an astropecten or margined sea star, had been wrenched out of its home in the sand beyond the surf by the storm. It, along with other sea stars, belongs to the phylum *Echinodermata*, an ancient group of animals that live exclusively in marine environments. Their ancestors, the crinoids or sea lilies, dwelt on stalks attached to the floor of Paleozoic seas hundreds of millions of years ago.

One of the most distinctive characteristics of the echinoderms is their radial symmetry, usually patterned around the number five. My tree-top ornament, with its five arms, or "rays," shares this trait with sea urchins, sand dollars, and a number of other sea stars and brittle stars, all of which belong to this phylum.

Another unique characteristic is the spiny outer coating, from which the name *Echinoderm*, or "hedgehog skin," is derived. This coating protects an inner skeleton which, in sea stars, is composed of tiny calcareous plates, known as ossicles, which form flexible joints.

Sea stars operate by means of a unique plumbing system known as a "water vascular system." Water is brought in through a perforated plate on the upper surface of the animal. A network of tubes carries the water throughout the body to a multitude of tubular "feet" on the bottom side. By varying the water pressure, the sea star can extend or contract the tube feet to move, breathe, and feed.

One of the most bizarre traits of some sea stars, including the common asteriids found all along the Atlantic coast, is the way they feed. Sea stars are predators, feeding mainly on worms, crustaceans, and bivalves, such as oysters and clams. Asteriids use their tube feet to pull open the two halves of bivalves, then pop their stomachs through their mouths and into the shell. The digestive juices in the

stomach liquidate the body of the victim, and cilia carry the dissolved shellfish into the sea star.

This habit makes this species very unpopular with fishermen who harvest oysters, clams, mussels and scallops. Oyster beds are particularly vulnerable to the voracious sea stars. One scientist described them as "gangsters of the deep in bullet-proof vests."

Early attempts to destroy asteriids by tearing them apart were abysmal failures. The disconnected rays regenerated, becoming entire sea stars. Instead of killing the pests, the fishermen sometimes created four new ones for each one they thought they had destroyed. The sea star's capacity to regenerate itself is due to an extremely complex nervous system described as "more complicated than the London telephone exchange."

Fishermen now use a "starfish mop," a bar covered with bundles of rope yarn that entangles sea stars. The mop is dragged from a boat until it is covered with starfish, then dipped into a vat of boiling water on deck. Suction dredges are also used to "vacuum" up the predators, after which they are buried. But even with modern technology, it is doubtful that sea star populations will decline any time soon. Not only are they tough and able to regenerate themselves, but they are also extremely prolific in reproduction.

Each spring, females eject thousands of eggs into the water, where they are fertilized by male sperm. Within months, the offspring have passed through their larval stage into tiny star-shaped organisms, ready to take their place in the marine ecosystem. Slowly and methodically, they prowl the sandy ocean floor, usually covering two to four miles a month, eating their way through life.

And sometimes, if they happen to wash onto the beach, they may bring a thrilling moment to some lucky child or adult who happens onto them. They may even find their way to the top of a Christmas tree.

The Sands of Time

Sand surrounded me. No longer was I aware of the crashing surf, the cloud-flecked sky, the crying of the gulls. Only the sand.

It rose on my left in rolling dunes covered with sea oats, forming a barrier between the ocean and the marshes. It stretched before me, a long silver ribbon melting into the distant horizon. On my right, it descended into the ocean, where it was battered and churned by the waves, disappearing out of sight beneath the restless waters. It lay behind me, now marked with the footprints impressed upon it by my bare feet.

Never before, in all my visits to the beach, had I really been aware of the sand. The colors and the textures changed with each step I took.

The white sand, which made up most of the beach, was quartz, an igneous rock formed deep underground. Closer to the water, the shades turned from white to caramel-brown. The sand here, known as "shell hash," was composed of calcium and aragonite. It was formed from the shells of millions of living creatures deep in the ocean. Higher up on the beach, near the dunes, were ribbons of black (magnetite and ilmenite) and deep red (garnet). The different sands blended together into a single panorama, which I knew as the Ocracoke beach.

Up on the dunes, the sands formed a substrate where plants could grow—sea rocket, beach grass, sea oats, and dune spurge. At the water's edge, it provided a home for coquina clams, mole crabs, and sand hoppers, which feed and bury themselves at the edge of the surf. The sands between the dunes and the surf provided protection for ghost crabs scurrying sideways from hole to hole in search of food.

The sand formed a feeding ground for the numerous birds that migrate along the beaches—sandpipers, plovers, and gulls. In the spring, it provided a place for oystercatchers and terns to scratch out shallow nests and lay their eggs. And in the summer it formed the arena where hundreds of beachgoers lay their towels to relax and gather the warm rays of the sun.

Where did the sands come from? How did they get here?

Many of the tiny grains had been carried here in rivers from the mainland millions of years ago. They formed other islands, long since disappeared. They became part of the ocean floor, lying buried deep within the sea for eons, before being shaped by the elements into the narrow barrier island where I now stood.

Before that, they had danced through the river beds, perhaps stopping somewhere along the way to become part of a lush, fern-draped savannah. Earlier, they formed part of the rough terrain blanketing the great mountains, the Appalachians, which extend like a backbone through the eastern United States. They were probably larger then—chunks of rock which some crayfish-like animal may have hidden under in a mountain stream, or which a dinosaur may have swallowed to aid in digesting its dinner.

Earlier still, before being broken apart by wind and weather, they may have been part of the mountain itself, a huge monolith protruding through the trees and reaching for the sky.

But go back even farther. The tiny grains of sand I was walking on lay deep below the surface of the earth once upon a time. They formed a boiling froth of magma trapped beneath the earth's crust. This liquid rock gradually cooled and solidified into the quartz, magnetite, and ilmenite that lay at my feet today.

And farther back than that?

The history of the sands on the beach go back to the beginning of time itself.

Some of the sands were formed in a very different way. They came from the ocean, where they had been tumbled and churned and tossed through a world of undulating seaweeds, giant whales, and minute zooplankton. These sands were the remnants of numerous species of mollusks that had once lived in the ocean: scallops, jingle shells, whelks, moonshells. Although the animals themselves were long gone, they had left behind their protective shells, to be eroded gradually into the tiny building blocks of the beach.

I closed my eyes, allowing my mind to be absorbed by the presence of the sands. As I did so, reality tilted. I was no longer standing on Ocracoke Island on an autumn day. I was standing on all of North Carolina—the river plains, the mountains, the bowels of the earth. My feet sank into the mysteries of the ocean depths, where millions of creatures had lived and died to form the floor beneath me. I was standing on a billion years of history.

As I stood with my eyes closed, reality shifted again. I saw the sands pouring slowly through a giant hourglass, and as I watched, I saw that the sands were running out. Then, just as the last grains of sand trickled through, I saw the hourglass turn, and the whole process began again—formation and destruction, birth and death, creation and extinction.

I opened my eyes and found myself once more on the beach at Ocracoke. I turned and looked behind me, watching as the wind and

Fall

the rising tide erased the footsteps I had left in the sand. As all traces of my passage disappeared, it occurred to me that my passing had not been obliterated. Rather, it had been absorbed, making me a part of the eloquent story hidden and preserved in the eternal sands of time.